The New English Grammar

by R. A. Close

ENGLISH AS A FOREIGN LANGUAGE

The New English Grammar

LESSONS IN ENGLISH AS A FOREIGN LANGUAGE

By R. A. CLOSE
British Council Representative, Athens

PARTS ONE AND TWO

LONDON
GEORGE ALLEN & UNWIN LTD
Ruskin House Museum Street

PRINTED IN GREAT BRITAIN
in 10/11 pt Times Roman type
BY HAZELL WATSON AND VINEY LTD
AYLESBURY, BUCKS

PREFACE

This book provides the essential grounding that all students of English need before they can understand and use the language properly. In its material, it includes important features of the English of today that are not dealt with in traditional textbooks. In its method, it avoids definitions, pedantic or specialist terminology and dubious 'rules', and concentrates on putting example into practice. Such new material and methods are already widely known and are rapidly replacing the old. This book makes them into a comprehensive course covering pronunciation, spelling, grammatical forms, sentence structure and idiom, and exercising essential vocabulary. An original contribution to English language teaching is made in the exercises on the articles, prepositions and tenses, following principles explained in the author's *English as a Foreign Language*.

Part One lays a basis for good pronunciation (including stress and intonation) and accurate spelling. Part Two deals with nouns, articles, adjectives, adjuncts, pronouns, verbs, tenses, adverbs, prepositions, the construction of the simple sentence, and word-order. Parts Three and Four follow.

This book was begun at Wedmore in Somerset, whose significance in the early history of the English language is a reminder that the roots of modern English are old and deep. It was finished on an island off the coast of Greece, in an atmosphere of clarity which I hope has penetrated into these pages. Certain obscurities in the typescript were removed through the painstaking efforts of Mr Andrew Bonar. I am responsible for those that remain. The passage quoted in Exercise 252 is from Ethel Manning's *The Flowery Sword* (Hutchinson) and that in Exercise 253 from a broadcast talk by Dr J. Welch on 'The Foundations of Western Values' (*The Listener*).

R. A. C.

EXPLANATION AND ADVICE TO TEACHERS

What is 'the new English grammar'?

To know and be able to speak and write any language well, we must have a perfect control of its grammar, by which I mean its own particular *system* of communication. Imagine the system as an intricate machine capable of conveying an immense variety of meanings, and making very subtle *distinctions* in meaning. The system is built up of a comparatively small number of words, parts of words, and speech-sounds, modified by stress, pitch and tone of voice. To understand and use the language, we must also know many other words that fit into the system, or that feed the machine and enable it to transmit and receive messages for a great variety of occasions.* The system works as a set of *conventions*, i.e. habits—in this case habits of speech or writing—adopted in a community by common consent. When we learn our mother tongue, we pick up these habits unconsciously, and they become engrained in us. In learning another language, we must—unless we have exceptional opportunities or powers of imitation—be taught them with the direct or indirect aid of a grammatical systematisation or *scheme*, i.e. the product of an attempt to trace and describe the system and to classify and label its component parts.

All that is true of English. Yet people often say that English is unsystematic; that grammar, as far as English is concerned, has practically disappeared, and that as a method it does not really help us to *learn* the language. That will appear to be true also, so long as we go on applying to English the kind of grammatical scheme that was meant to describe the underlying system of, say, Latin or Anglo-Saxon. But modern English can be systematised in its own right. It will then be found to have plenty of grammar of its own kind. If the teaching of English through grammar has failed, there are two reasons for it. First, much of what has been taught as English grammar is dead wood, or dogma passed on by one generation of pedagogues to another, while significant features of the living language have been overlooked. Secondly, we have paid too much attention to *knowing a scheme*, with its definitions, rules and terminology; and too little to gaining *control of the system*. What the great majority of students want and need is not so much to know the grammar as to speak and

---

* It would be a waste of time for a student to try or be expected to learn a large assortment of words without being able to control the system on which their effective use depends; and it would help the student if he realised from the beginning that he can and need only learn a limited amount of the vocabulary of a major language, according to his requirements.

write grammatically. They want to be able to work the machine, not merely to learn a design of it.

The 'new English grammar', therefore, might refer to the significant features of modern English; or to the natural arrangement of them in a system; or to a logical systematisation of them. Many of them are survivals from the past; others may be recent developments; all must belong to the English of the twentieth century. The term 'new English grammar' might also refer to a teaching method that keeps definitions and rules in the background and concentrates on training in conventional usage.

This is a textbook for the teaching of the new English grammar in this modern way. It is designed as a course of training in the handling of a complex system of communication; and it supplies a stock of vocabulary that we shall often want to feed into the machine for purposes of social intercourse and scientific statement.

For Whom is this Course Intended?

The course is intended for two main categories of student:
(a) intelligent beginners able and wishing to become proficient in both the spoken and the written language, for their general education or for some special purpose; and
(b) more advanced students (including prospective and practising teachers) who want or need a reference book or a remedial course broadly covering the fundamentals of their subject.

Beginners will require a tutor to explain meanings; and both categories of student should have a tutor (or a good recording of at least the first part of the course) to give reliable models of pronunciation. Notes, and a key to certain of the exercises, are provided for teachers. The notes and key can also be used by students working on their own.

Its Aims

Students using the course are expected to think, to think what they are doing, and to think in English from the start. Their *ultimate aim* should be to give their undivided attention to *meaning*, to comprehend what they hear and read in English, and to express themselves effectively in it. To achieve that aim, they must understand how the grammatical system works and learn to operate it correctly and unconsciously. Their *immediate aim* should therefore be to become so automatically proficient in the mechanics of the language as to be able to concentrate on meaning and style. It is very hard to think of the meaning and the mechanics at the same time.

What do we Mean by 'Correct'?

Users of this course are expected to speak and write 'correctly'. But what do we mean by that? In this course, 'correctness' should be seen primarily as a matter of *effective communication*, i.e. a process through which the hearer (or reader) understands precisely what the speaker (or writer) intends to convey. Whether a word or construction is 'correct' depends on (*a*) just what the speaker has in mind and tries to express, and where he wants to place his emphasis; and (*b*) his choosing the precise form of expression conventionally associated with his particular shade of meaning. A hearer or reader understands correctly when he sees exactly what the speaker or writer means. In order to speak or write English correctly ourselves, the essential thing is that we should express our meaning in such a way that our audience or our readers understand it fully and precisely if they know English perfectly and are relying on no other medium.

In taking part in this process of communication, either as sender or receiver, we must know and use the conventions of which the system we are handling is composed. Without strict observance of these conventions, a language would soon cease to function as a means of social intercourse. The conventions either have meaning in themselves, or help us make a distinction in meaning, so that if we ignore or mis-use them we may not succeed in expressing our exact meaning effectively.* Moreover, mis-use of them will turn our audience's attention towards our mistakes and away from our meaning: it may even alienate people's sympathy so that they refuse to listen to what we have to say. For these reasons, conformity with the current conventions of the language we are learning is not only desirable but is also more or less essential to complete comprehension.

'Correctness' should therefore be seen as a matter of effective communication, and that is dependent on conformity with widely adopted habits of speech and writing. 'In*correctness' is then a matter of failure in the communication of meaning, and this may result from ignorance or mis-use of the conventions. The teacher should realise that there are degrees of seriousness in 'mistakes', depending on the degree of the student's failure to make his exact meaning clear to somebody relying entirely on English.

---

* For example, the habit in English of using the word *the*, as in *Give me the paper*, is a convention expressing the meaning 'that specimen, or those specimens of paper, or that object of a special kind made of paper, which the speaker assumes the hearer can identify'. This convention would be used quite unconsciously by people whose mother-tongue is English, but not so by a Russian, Chinese or Japanese, for whom at first it would be a mystery.

Now there may be more than one widely adopted habit in the pronunciation, spelling or function of an English word, and consequently there are **varieties** of English. All important varieties follow the same basic patterns, since they are all recognisably 'English'. If you master the system of one of the major varieties, you should have no difficulty in making the comparatively minor adjustments necessary to understand another variety and to make yourself understood in it. Learners with limited time for studying English need to concentrate on one of its more widely accepted varieties, and even that must be standardised for purposes of study. This book reflects a standardisation, by a student and teacher of grammar, of the kind of English with which he happens to have grown familiar.* He expects his readers *not* to assume that other widely accepted forms of English are 'wrong', or in any sense less desirable than his own. He would regard as 'wrong' a linguistic specimen which is supposed to be English, which has some of the characteristics of it, but which would not be fully accepted as English in any one of its generally adopted forms. However, an accepted expression which is peculiar to one form of English may be 'unsuitable' when it occurs in a context of a different style.

Make sure you can do all the exercises in this course yourself, and get them right. Your pupils can learn more from your example, for good or ill, than from the book.

Rules

'Correctness' should not necessarily be taken to mean 'obedience to stated rules'. You must not conclude from this that in English we can do what we like: we are bound by the necessity of expressing our meaning effectively, and, in doing that, of conforming to the conventions. But the conventions of English are not defined as rules laid down by any authority. The only real authorities for English usage are tradition and common consent, whose rules are found reflected in what people actually say and write. Your best guide to 'correct' English is not a book of 'rules' but the example of authentic English, in a full context, spoken or written by people who can express themselves effectively, and who follow widely adopted practice. Teachers and textbook writers often **invent** rules, which their students and readers repeat and perpetuate. These rules are usually statements about English usage which the authors imagine to be, *as a rule*, true.

* The writer was born and educated in southern England, and has spent most of his adult life in academic or administrative circles, either in London or in international communities abroad where English has been a common tongue.

But statements of this kind are extremely difficult to formulate both simply and accurately. They are rarely altogether true; often only partially true; sometimes contradicted by usage itself. Sometimes the contrary to them is also true.* They must therefore sooner or later be supplemented and supported by a patch-work of sub-rules and exceptions. Learning rules of this kind can be largely a waste of time: it must not be mistaken for learning English or even for learning its grammar.

Instead of trusting to so-called rules, the student should be encouraged to rely on:

(a) typical *examples* of English usage, particularly when those follow *patterns* of a high degree of usefulness and when they occur or can be used in real situations or context; and

(b) *advice* on what to do in certain circumstances. Definite pieces of advice are much safer than sweeping generalisations and should not be converted into them. They should be based on a clear understanding of the language and should not be issued or learnt in the abstract. They should be related to specific examples and put into practice as soon as they are given.

Warning: This book gives information and advice. It is not the author's intention to lay down a code of laws.

Explanations

Certain explanations are given in this book, especially in the Notes, for the guidance of teachers and advanced students. Teachers should resist the temptation of passing these explanations on to pupils in the early stages: let learners give their attention chiefly to the examples and the exercises. In any case, beware of explanations, as of rules. It is extremely difficult, perhaps impossible, to explain *why* we say what we do; and it is by no means easy even to define the circumstances in which we say it. The time devoted to abstract (and often unsatisfactory) explanations of usage can often be much better spent observing usage in an interesting context, and imitating it in practice.

None the less, teachers will always want to give *some* explanation of usage, if only because students will always demand it; and every textbook writer assumes *to a certain extent* that he can provide it. The present writer is no exception; and readers will find in his *English as a Foreign Language* the assumptions on which many of the exercises in the following pages have been based. The writer does not expect everyone to agree with those assumptions; but at least

* See *English as a Foreign Language* by R. A. Close (George Allen and Unwin, London, 1962).

they provide a carefully laid foundation on which to place his examples: and *it is the examples that the pupils should learn, practise and imitate.*

Choice of Material

In learning a language it is important to maintain a proper *balance* of its main elements in the cultivation of the different skills required. This consideration has determined the choice of material in these pages and the order of its presentation. Students should follow this order strictly, working through each exercise in turn, even though they may 'know' it, or think they do.

The *vocabulary* used is primarily *structural*, i.e. consisting of words required for the construction of sentences of various kinds, whatever the subject-matter. Secondly, it consists of *content* words in very frequent use, or words of lower frequency but of a high degree of usefulness. The choice of vocabulary has been influenced particularly by *A General Service List of English Words* (Dr Michael West, Longmans Green, London, 5th Edition, 1960), and by the lists worked out by Mr C. K. Ogden and Professor I. A. Richards in their fundamental researches into words and meanings.

The selection of the *syntax patterns* introduced in this course and the order of their presentation were determined by the scheme outlined in the Contents. This was done solely because the present writer decided to deal with the problem in that way: which for practical purposes and in the present state of our knowledge is perhaps an adequate reason.

The Exercises: Practise Language like Music

The exercises are not, of course, meant for translation, but for *practice in English*. Their technique has been influenced by the work of several modern British and American linguists, and by the author's feeling that learning to operate the machinery of language is like learning to play a musical instrument. Like music, language has rhythm and tune and is made up of sounds and symbols which have no meaning unless they are put together in certain arrangements. Both are composed of a great variety of patterns and variations on them. Each requires several skills which must be synchronised and executed automatically, so that the performer can give his full attention to expression and meaning. For both, it is not the theory but the performance that counts; and each therefore demands constant practice.

Focus attention in each exercise on its main purpose. However, even a short sentence, like a bar of music, may contain several patterns that cannot be separated. While you are concentrating on one pattern, you may also be using others which have either occurred in previous exercises, or not. In other words, you will incidentally be reviewing, or previewing. Reviewing is essential to language learning, and it is often best done incidentally. Previewing is also important. It prepares us for the future, so that a new lesson supplies something we are waiting to hear.

What Else do You Need?

Any course such as this must be accompanied by conversation and reading where the words and constructions introduced in the course are used in a genuine context. Only in context can we see the full meaning of words, and discover their exact *field* of meaning. This course is, after all, only a preparation for real English, i.e. not the simplified and standardised language of the language lesson, but English that is spoken and written by native speakers of it in normal communication. The student will soon reach a point where progress can be made not by doing more and more 'grammar', but by reading and using real English in pursuit of what interests him. In any case, not until he experiences grammar, and puts it into practice, in a genuine and interesting *context*, can his command of it stand a chance of becoming perfect.

You will, of course, need a good dictionary, not only to explain meanings but also as a guide to spelling, pronunciation and established usage. You will find that works such as the *Pronouncing Dictionary* of Professor Daniel Jones, the *Advanced Learner's Dictionary of Current English* by Hornby, Gatenby and Wakefield (Oxford University Press), the *Concise Oxford Dictionary* and Webster's *Collegiate Dictionary* contain much of the information you will need about the language as you proceed with your studies.

R. A. C.

The use of the accents, which indicate stress and intonation, should become quite clear as one works systematically through the book, following the notes and paying particular attention to the explanation given on page 166.

CONTENTS

CONTENTS

Contents

Part Three will contain:

Part Four.

PART ONE

THE SYSTEM OF PRONUNCIATION AND SPELLING

---

1. THE SOUND AND SPELLING OF ENGLISH WORDS

The Sounds of English

TABLE 1

The English Vowels

Number	Key Word	Number	Key Word
1	**see**	13	**day**
2	this	14	**time**
3	pen	15	**boy**
4	that		
5	**car**	16	**house**
6	hot	17	**home**
7	**horn**		
8	look	18	**here**
9	**moon**	19	**hair**
10	sun	*Where the key word is in*	
11	**burn**	*heavy type, pronounce the*	
12	(bèt)ter	*vowel* **long.**	

EXERCISE 1. *Learn and practise Table 1.*

2. *LISTEN; then give the number of each* **vowel** *sound:*

(a) one, two, three, four, five, six, seven, eight, nine, ten, eleven, twelve, thirteen, fourteen, fifteen, sixteen, seventeen, eighteen, nineteen, twenty.

(b) Do you speak English? No, but I am learning it.

(c) I want to learn English. You are learning it now.

(d) I am, you are; I was, you were; boy, girl.

(e) man, men; woman, women; child, children.

(f) Learn and practise Table One. The English vowels.

(g) Number, key word. Exercise two. Listen to each sound.

(h) This is number eight. Is this number ten?

(*i*) No it is not. It is nought. Very good. Thank you.
(*j*) Please sit down. Say that after me. Say it again.

3. *LISTEN; then give the number of each vowel sound:*
   (*a*) live, leave. Where do you live? In this street.
   (*b*) feel, fill. Feel this wood. Is it rough or smooth?
   (*c*) still, steel; sheep, ship; heat, hit, head, hat.
   (*d*) bed, bad, board, bird; run, ran; angry, hungry.
   (*e*) sharp, shop, shot, short, shut; weak, ankle, walk, uncle.
   (*f*) work, word, wide; high, low; law, order.
   (*g*) was, wars; day, die; why, way; wait, wet.
   (*h*) nice, nose, noise; he hears; we wear. Good idea.
   (*i*) full moon, soon; two chairs; three cheers.
   (*j*) How many cups? Thirteen. How much water?
   (*k*) Not much. Have you a match? Only one, no more. [100]

TABLE 1a

20 (or 7)	**more**	22	**fire**
21	**tour**	23	**power**

---

4. *Practise Table 1a. Then listen, and give the number of each vowel sound:*
   (*a*) twenty-one, twenty-two, twenty-three, twenty-four.
   (*b*) door; why, wire; too, poor; town, tower; tie, tired.
   (*c*) mine, yours, ours, theirs; floor, flower; fly, flyer.
   (*d*) tyre, burst, car, crash, iron, crush.

5. *Listen again to the words in Exercises 2, 3 and 4. Then say and REPEAT them clearly.*

6. *Practise pairs of vowels which you find difficult.*

7. *Learn and practise Table 2.*

8. *Listen to each* **word** *or syllable; then say the sound of the* **cönsonant** (*or the number of the vowel*) *at the beginning of it, and give the key word for that sound. Examples:* good:— g, garden; wood:— w, we; write:— r, run:
   (*a*) What is your name? Write that on paper.
   (*b*) Our next lesson is tomorrow at ten. Don't be late.
   (*c*) What is the key word for vowel number seven?
   (*d*) Whose is this thing? Did you say 'sing' or 'finger'?
   (*e*) right, wrong; light, dark; raw, rice; law, rule.

TABLE 2

The English Consonants
(single sounds)

Soft			Hard	
Sound	Key Words		Sound	Key Words
b	burn	—	p	pen
m	moon			
w	we			
v	voice	—	f	full
th(soft)	this	—	th(hard)	thing
d	day	—	t	table
n	no			
l	look, pull			
r	run			
z	zoo, pens	—	s	see, books
[ʒ]	measure	—	sh	ship
y	yes			
g	garden	—	k	cake
ng	long			
h	here			

(*f*) loud shout; soft voice; town, village; down there.

(*g*) good girl; fair, hair; he thinks; she speaks; one, do.

(*h*) warm air; fine weather; vine, wine; heat, sheet; sort, short.

(*i*) think, sink; thought, fought; sure, sugar; no use.

(*j*) push, bull; bush, pull. He shows, she sews.

9. **Twelve** (*one syllable*). **Twenty** (*two syllables*). *Listen to each word. Do you hear one syllable, or two? Is the last sound a consonant, or a vowel? What consonant or vowel is the last sound?*

(*a*) rub, rubber; stopper, stop; some, summer; love, lover.

(*b*) leave, leaf; bath, bathe, bather; ride, write, rider, writer.

(*c*) rice, rise; place, plays; runner, run; bag, pack.

(*d*) crash, garage; study, student; live, lived; stop, stopped.

(*e*) song, sing; singing, singer; strong, stronger; English; ended.

10. *Listen to each group of words in Exercises 8 and 9, then say and repeat it correctly.*

11. **Pràctise:** pull, bull, tàble, pèople (1), sỳllable (2), lìttle, pèncil, gèntle, gèntlemen, sìngle, doùble (10), bìcycle (14), ùncle, ànkle,

pòssible, tèrrible (3), còmfortable (10); sun, sèven (3), listen, òften, lèsson, gàrden, cùshion (8), attèntion, stàtion (13), translàtion.

TABLE 3

The English Consonants
(compound sounds, and clusters)

First sound soft		*First sound hard*
jump	—	chair
drink	—	tree
blue	—	please
brown	—	print
		flat
		front
		three
glad	—	cloud
green	—	cream
		twelve
		quick
		six
	First sound hard	
small	swim	street
speak	snow	scout, sky
split	sleep	square
spring	stop	screw

---

12. *Practise Table 3. Then* **lísten** *and* **repèat:**

(a) John, George; Charles, church; Mary, Jane; English language.
(b) sleep, dream; slip, slope; dry, try; train, drain.
(c) bright blue; below, blow; play, pray; please, police.
(d) present, past; pleasant journey; fly, fry; three, free.
(e) great crowd; clean glass; green grass; grease-proof.
(f) twice twenty; quite quiet; exercise six; throw, threw.
(g) sweet smile; speak slowly; stand still; sneeze, splash.
(h) sport, support; straight line; strong tea; strange people.
(i) skin, scratch; lost, found; count, most; thank, thanks.
(j) jumps, jumped; round table; bags, packs; men's clothes.

13. *Listen, and* **pronöunce** *all these words with the sounds* $y + 9$:

(a) you, use, ùseful, unìted, univèrsity;
(b) beaùtiful, pure, mùsic; view, few; due, dùty, new tune, Tùesday, stùdent; excùse, hùmour, hùman, huge.

Syllables: Accented and Unaccented

14. *Listen, and repeat:*

(*a*) Ēng-lish; nùm-ber; pràct-ise; lìs-ten, èx-er-cise.

(*b*) beaù-ti-ful; mùs-ic; to-dày; to-mòr-row; yès-ter-day.

(*c*) mòrn-ing; äf-ter-nòon; èven-ing; Mòn-day; Tùes-day.

(*d*) Wèdnes-day; Thùrs-day; Frì-day; Sàt-ur-day; Sùn-day.

(*e*) thïr-tèen; thìr-ty; föur-tèen; fòr-ty; fïf-tèen; fìf-ty.

(*f*) phò-to-graph; pho-tò-graph-er; phö-to-gràph-ic; äp-par-à-tus.

(*g*) ex-plàin; èx-plan-à-tion; pro-nòunce; pro-nünc-i-à-tion.

(*h*) know; knòw-ledge; àc-cid-ent; äc-cid-ènt-al-ly.

(*i*) còm-fort-a-ble; ärm-chàir; ràd-i-o; të-le-vì-sion.

(*j*) rè-cord; re-còrd; òb-ject; ob-jèct; im-pòrt-ant, nèc-ess-ary.

How English Words are Written

TABLE 4
The English Alphabet

Printed		Written		Pronunciation
Capital	*small letter*	*Capital*	*small letter*	
A	a	*𝒜 or 𝒶*	*a*	ay (*as in* say)
B	b	*ℬ*	*b*	bee
C	c	*𝒞 or C*	*c*	see
D	d	*𝒟*	*d*	dee
E	e	*ℰ*	*e*	ee (*as in* see)
F	f	*ℱ*	*f*	ef
G	g	*𝒢*	*g*	jee
H	h	*ℋ or H*	*h*	aitch
I	i	*ℐ*	*i*	i (*as in* time)
J	j	*𝒥*	*j*	jay
K	k	*𝒦*	*k*	kay
L	l	*ℒ*	*l*	el
M	m	*ℳ or M*	*m*	em
N	n	*𝒩*	*n*	en
O	o	*𝒪*	*o*	o (*as in* home)
P	p	*𝒫*	*p*	pee
Q	q	*𝒬*	*q*	kyoo
R	r	*ℛ*	*r or r*	ar
S	s	*𝒮 or 𝒮*	*s*	es

23

TABLE 4: The English Alphabet—*continued*

Printed		Written		Pronunciation
Capital	small letter	Capital	small letter	
T	t	*Y*	*t*	tee
U	u	*U*	*u*	yoo
V	v	*V*	*v*	vee
W	w	*W*	*w*	double-yoo
X	x	*X*	*x*	eks
Y	y	*Y*	*y*	wy
Z	z	*Z*	*z*	zed

15. *Learn the English* **àlphabet. CÖPY** (6) *the wrïtten* (2) *lètters. Then copy the key words in Tables 1, 1a, 2 and 3 in English wrìting* (14). *Say each word as you copy it. Do the same with Exercise 14, but join all the letters of one word together, without hỳphens* (14).

16. **SPELL:** table (tee, ay, bee, el, ee), see (es, double-e), look, better, why, house, fire. *Learn the* **spelling** *of all the words in Tables 1, 1a, 2, 3 and 4.*

TABLE 5

The Spelling of English Vowel Sounds
(standard)

1	see, sea, me, these	13	say, rain, date
2	pin, *y* in vèry (3)	14	why, fine, high, I
3	pen	15	boy, noise
4	hat	16	house, how
5	car	17	note, coat, no, toe
6	not	18	cheer, here, hear
7	horn, law	19	chair, care
8	look	20	more, door
9	too, June, blue, new	21	pure, fewer
10	sun	22	fire, higher
11	her, first, burn	23	our, flower
12	*Second syllable in* bètter, àctor, còllar		

Reading: English Vowels

17. *Learn Table 5: THIS IS A SCHEME FOR THE SPELLING OF ENGLISH VOWEL SOUNDS AND THE PRONUNCIATION OF VOWEL LETTERS. Then* **READ** *the following:*

24

(*a*) Free, meet, need; speak, read, teach; he, she; complète, scene, scheme.

(*b*) Big, fish, ship; hàppy, fùnny. Bètter, best, sell, well.

(*c*) Cat, flat, match, stand. Arm, bar, hard, sharp.

(*d*) Dog, got, lot, top. Short, sort, sport; law, raw, saw.

(*e*) Book, cook, hook, took. Soon, spoon, food, school, shoot, smooth; tune; true; few, view.

(*f*) But, bùtter, cup, cut, shut. Bird, girl, shirt; turn, hurt.

(*g*) Lètter, nùmber, vìsitor, gràmmar; addrèss, alòne, accòunt.

(*h*) Day, may, play; wait, pain, plain; face, make, late.

(*i*) Dry, try, fly; bite, hide, nice; bright, light, night.

(*j*) Toy; coin, point, spoil. Loud, mouth, shout; now, down, town.

(*k*) Bone, nose, stone; boat, road, soap; go, so.

(*l*) Beer, steer; ear, dear, near, tear, year. Fair, hair, stair.

(*m*) stare, share, spare. Shore, tore, wore; floor.

(*n*) Cure, endùre. Higher, hire, wire. Flour, flower, power, tower.

18. *Important exceptions to the scheme in Table 5. Read the words in this Exercise with the vowel sound indicated at the beginning of each line:*

		Key Word	Other examples
a	5	fàther	àfter; half; dance, branch, ànswer, can't, plant; ask, class, glass, grass, pass; last, past, fàsten, nàsty; bath, path, ràther. (*See note*)
(w)a	6	want	was, wash, watch, what; *also* wand, wànder; quàlity, quàntity.
al, (w)ar	7	all, war	ball, hall, small, tall, wall; alrèady, àlso, àlways; salt, talk, walk; ward, warm, quàrter.
ea	3	bread	brèakfast, dead, deaf, death, head, health, lèather, mèasure, plèasure, ready.
	13	great	break, steak.
ear, }	11	èarly	earn, earth, learn.
ere }	19	wear, where	bear, pear, tear; there.
o	9	do	to, two, who.
	10	come	bròther, còlour, còmfortable, còmpany, còver, done, front, Lòndon, love, Mònday, mòney, month, mòther, none, nòthing, one,* òther, some, son, stòmach, ton, tongue, won, wònder.

* *Pronounce as* [wun].

		Key Word	Other examples
oo	8	**good**	foot, room, wood, wool.
(w)or	11	**word**	work, world, worm, worse, worst, worth.
ow	17	**know**	grow, show, snow, sow (*seed*), throw; bow.
u	8	**full**	bull, bush, pull, push, put.

19. *Read the following* **sèntences.** *Then copy them, saying each word as you* **write** *it:*

(*a*) Be here at five. Do not be late. Don't (17) be late.
(*b*) Please stand up. Sit down again. Wait for me.
(*c*) Stop talking. What is your name? I can't hear.
(*d*) How old are (5) you (9)? I am sïxtèen, not sìxty.
(*e*) What is the key (1) word for vowel number two?
(*f*) Show me your book. What does (10) this word mean?
(*g*) I don't know. I can't ünderstànd. Explàin it to me.
(*h*) We want to learn Ènglish (2). Learn this by heart (5).
(*i*) My bröther is a stùdent (y + 9). He is stüdying (10) làw.
(*j*) Göod-býe (8 + 14). I hope you have (4) a plëasant (3) joùrney (11). Come back soon.

Reading: English Consonants.

20. *Pronounce and learn the examples below. THESE EXAMPLES, COMBINED WITH THOSE IN TABLE 2, PROVIDE A SCHEME FOR THE PRONUNCIATION OF WRITTEN CONSONANTS.*

Letter	Sound	Examples
c	k	cat, come, cup.
	s (*before e, i*)	cent, cìty (2).
cc	k	occàsion (13), accòunt, occùr.
	ks (*before e, i*)	accèpt, àccident.
ch	ch	chair, cheese, chin, choose.
ck	k	quick, lock, luck.
g	g	game, good, gun.
	j (*before e, i, y*)	gèneral, gìnger, Ègypt (1 + 2).
gh	Silent*	high, light, night; straight; through (9), though (17).
gu	g	guard, guess, guest, tongue.
h	h	hair, he, here, hit, house, hunt.
kn	n (k silent)	knee, knife, know (17), knòwledge (6).
ph	f	phòtograph, phỳsics (2).

* *Except at the beginning of a word, when it is pronounced g, as in* ghost (17).

26

Letter	Sound	Examples
pn	*p silent*	pneumònia (*see note*).
ps	*p silent*	psychòlogy (*see note*).
qu	*kw*	quàrter, queen, quiet (22).
s	*z in* / *s in*	boys, girls, pens, pèncils, goes. / shops, hats, books, puts.
-sion	*[ʒ] + n in* / *sh + n in*	occàsion, tëlevìsion (*after a vowel*). / pènsion, tènsion (*after a consonant*).
th	*th, soft*	the, this, that, then, there; fàther, mòther, bròther, òther; bathe, breathe (1), smooth, with.
	th, hard	thank, thick, thin, thing, think; bath, path, breath (3); nòthing.
-tion	*sh + n*	attèntion, addìtion, cömposìtion, stàtion.
wh	*w in*	what, when, where, which, why.
wr	*w silent*	write, wrong, wrap, wreck, wrist.

Exceptions:

b	*silent in*	climb (14), comb (17), debt, doubt, dumb, thumb.
ch	*k in*	school, stòmach, chàracter (4), àrchitect, chèmistry, psychòlogy.
	sh in	machìne (1).
g	*g in*	get, give, gift, girl.
gh	*f in*	laugh (5), cough (6), enoùgh (10), rough (10).
gu	*gw in*	lànguage.*
h	*silent in*	hònest (6), hònour (6), hour.
s	*sh in*	sùgar (8), sure.
s	*[ʒ] in*	plèasure, mèasure, ùsual (9).
sc	*s (c silent) in*	science (22), scissors, scene.
t	*silent in*	lìsten, fàsten, càstle, whìstle, *and commonly in* òften.
w	*silent in*	two, ànswer, sword (7).
wh	*h in*	who, whose (9), whole.

21. *Listen. Read: then* **learn by heart** *and write out from* **memory:**

There are fïve pëople (1) in our fàmily (4) | —Fáther, Móther, my bróther, my síster and mysèlf. We lïve (2) in a smäll hóuse | jüst outsïde the tòwn. Sömè people lïve in fláts, or apàrtments. We have a lärge gárden, | with früit (9)-trees and flòwers. My fäther and bróther

* *Pronounce as* [làngwidge].

| gö to wörk in an öffice. My sïster göes to schóol, | and I gö to the üniversity. Möther stäys at hòme äll däy.

22. *Listen. Repeat each sentence, or part of a long sentence, without looking at the book. Then read:*

(a) Göod mòrning. Höw àre you? Dïd you slëep wéll?

(b) I am vëry wéll, thànk yoú. I feel müch bètter.

(c) Whëre is your (7) bröther Hènry todäy? Is he at hóme?

(d) I have nö idèa (14 + 18). I thïnk he has göne (6) òut.

(e) Dïd you sëe mäny (3) pëople at the cóncert?

(f) Yès. I saw äll my öld schòol frïends (3) agäin.

(g) Coüld (8) you cöme to my höuse for téa on Thürsday?

(h) With plèasure. I will mäke a nöte of it nòw.

(i) Whät tìme is it? Nëarly hälf päst èight (13).

(j) It is töo èarly to go höme yét. I have some möre wòrk to dö.

(k) Whö is thère? Spëak ùp. I cän't hëar your vòice.

(l) I wänt to büy (14) some bréad, méat, végetables, sált, sùgar.

(m) Whëre is the Töwn Hàll? Sträight ón, | thën türn lèft.

(n) Drïve through the gáte, | and pärk in the sìde strëet.

(o) Bë quìet. Stöp làughing. Öpen your bòoks. G̊o on wòrking.

(p) Wrïte càrefully. Is thïs wörd ríght or wròng?

(q) Gïve (2) me äll your attèntion. Änswer my quèstion.*

(r) My fäther säw the àccident. He gäve an accòunt of it to the polìce (1). He sáid (3), 'I säw whät hàppened.'*

(s) Ïs this störy trúe? I'm quìte sùre it is. There's nö döubt abòut it.

(t) Höw much möney do you ëarn in a mònth? Nòthing yét, I'm önly (17) a stùdent.

23. *Prepare Exercises 19, 21 and 22 for* **dictàtion.**

24. *Read the words in Exercises 2, 3, 4, 8, 9, 11, 12 and 13. Read the words in Exercise 14, first very carefully, syllable by syllable, then more fluently.*

Stressed and Unstressed Words in a Sentence

25. *Listen; and repeat, first deliberately, then fluently. Give the words in italics a weak* **pronünciàtion.**

	strong	weak	
a	13	12	Thïs is *a* pèn.
an	4	12	Thïs is *an* àpple.

* *In* question, *pronounce* -tion *as* ch + n. Happened, *two syllables.*

28

	strong	*weak*	
is	2 (+ z)	*s only*	Thät *is a* bòok. (That's . . .)
is	2 (+ z)	*z only*	Hëre *is a* pèncil. (Here's . . .)
the	1	12	Thät *is the* dòor. (That's . . .)
the	1	2	Whät *is the* ànswer?
to	9	12	Gö *to the* wìndow.
to	9	8	Gö *to a* dòctor.
am	4	12, *or m only*	}I *am* göing *for a* wàlk. (I'm . . .)
for	7	12	
it is	2, 2 + z	2 + s	} It *is* làte. We *must* gò. (It's . . .)
must	10	12	
but	10	12	*But* it's töo èarly *to* lëave yét.
are	5	12	Wë *are* göing *to* swìm. (We're . . .)
us	10 (+ s)	12 (+ s)	*Are* yoü cöming wíth *us*, |
	(After let, s *only*)		
them	3	12	or göing with thèm? Lët *us* sèe. (Let's . . .)
and	4	12	Häts *and* cóats, shöes (9) *and* sòcks.
can	4	12	Ï *can* sëe *a* shìp. Can yoú sëe it? Yës, I càn.
than	4	12	Yoü *can* see bëtter *than* Ì can.
some	10	12	Söme people lïve in flàts. Hëre *are some* lètters.
at	4	12	Büy stämps *at the* pòst-öffice (17, 6, 2).
have	4	12 (*or simply v*)	Häve you äny (3) stámps?
has (z)	4	12 (*or simply z*)	Ï *have* nòne (I've none), nör *has* Jòhn (6). (Nor's John.)

26. *Repeat fluently:*

This is a pen.	This is an apple.
That is the door.	What is the answer?
I can see a ship.	We are going to swim.

Make up sentences on these patterns, replacing the last word of each sentence by one of the following:
book, page, word, desk, chair, floor, cèiling (1), wall, window; arm, egg, òrange (6 + 2), umbrèlla; question, number, time; sleep, work, leave, stop.

Rhythm

27. *Listen; practise, and learn by heart:*

   (*a*) Bëtter läte *than* nèver (3). (*Proverb*)
   (*b*) *The* ëarly bïrd cätches *the* wòrm. (*Proverb*)
   (*c*) *A* bïrd in *the* hánd | is worth twö in *the* bùsh. (*Proverb*)
   (*d*) Täke *the* büll by *the* hòrns. (*Idiomatic saying*)
   (*e*) Thïs little pïg went *to* márket,
       Thïs little pïg stayed *at* hòme. (*Nursery Rhyme*)
   (*f*) Is thïs *the* fäce that läunched (7)* *a* thöusand shíps? (*Marlowe*)
   (*g*) *To* bé, or nòt *to* be, | — | thät is *the* quèstion. (*Shakespeare*)
   (*h*) If Wïnter cómes, *can* Sprïng be fär behínd? (14) (*Shelley*)
   (*i*) My heärt (5) is lïke *a* sïnging bìrd. (*Christina Rossetti*)
   (*j*) Is there änybody (3) thére? said *the* Träveller (4),
       Knöcking on *the* möonlit dóor. (*Walter de la Mare*)

Pitch and Íntonàtion: (1) Falling Tone

Examples

28. (*a*) (What is that?)   Food.   (stàtement)

    (*b*)   Wait!   (commànd)

    (*c*)   Why?   (quèstion)

Say the following on a falling tone:

   (*a*) Bread. Rice. Fruit. Milk. Tea. Yes. No. Now.
   (*b*) Stop! Run! Walk! Jump! Laugh! Cough! Help!
   (*c*) What? Who? Whose? Where? When? How?

29. *Practise the following examples with the intonation indicated at the beginning of each line:*

Wàter (7)   Garden. City. Study. Student. English.
                Question. Answer. Thirty. Forty. Fifty. Sixty.
                Monday. Tuesday. Wednesday. Thursday.
                Listen. Read it. Write it.

Beaùtiful   Exercise (3, 12, 14). Yesterday. Saturday.
                Accident. Traveller. Comfortable. Look at it.
                All of it.

* *Pronounce as* [lornsht].

A bòok . ❜ A hat. A coat. It's mine. The door. The wall. Some tea. Alone. Address. Towards (7).

Some wàter . ● . A student. A lawyer. My father. Your mother. Some people. An answer. I'm looking.

A phòtograph ● ● ● An exercise. A fountain-pen. A bi- cycle. An accident. Impossible.

It's a càr. . . ❜ At the door. I'm alone. In the room. I'm surprised.

It's a plèasure. ● . ● . I'm a student. He's a lawyer. She's attractive (12, 4, 2). In the garden.

30. *Phrases and sentences with more than one stress. Practise the examples with the intonation indicated:*

Gö hòme. ● ❜ Don't (17) wait. Why not? Stand still. Thirteen. Armchair.

Gö awày. ● . ❜ Come at once. Afternoon. Thirty- three. Forty-four. What is this?

Cöme to my ròom. ● . ❜ How do you do? Tell me the truth (9). What is the time? Why are you late?

Cöme quìckly. ● ● . Hot water. Young children (2). Old people. Speak slowly.

Whät a pìty! ● ● . What's the matter? Bring some water. Do it quickly.

Höw wònderful! ● ● . . What time is it? Take care of it.

I dön't knòw. ● . ❜ I can't see. An old man.

Whëre are you gòing? ● . ● . Why are you leaving?

Bëtter läte than nèver.   English words are easy.

The ëarly bïrd cätches the wòrm.

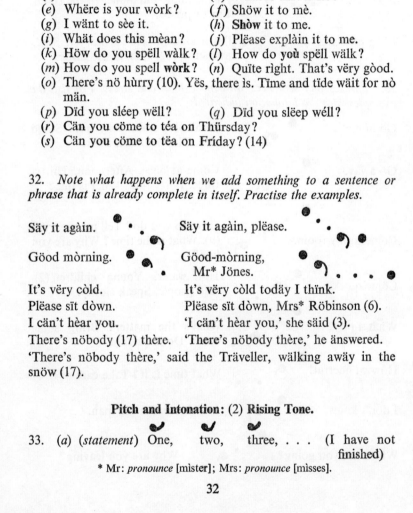

31. *Read the following. Notice which words are stressed, and give a special stress to the words in heavy type.*

(a) Thïs is a pìcture.

(b) And **thàt** is a pïcture.

(c) Whät is thät nòise?

(d) What is that **nòise**?

(e) Whëre is your wòrk?

(f) Shöw it to mè.

(g) I wänt to sèe it.

(h) **Shòw** it to me.

(i) Whät does this mèan?

(j) Plëase explàin it to me.

(k) Höw do you spëll wàlk?

(l) How do **yoù** spëll wälk?

(m) How do you spell **wòrk**?

(n) Quïte rìght. That's vëry gòod.

(o) There's nö hùrry (10). Yës, there ìs. Tïme and tïde wäit for nò män.

(p) Dïd you slèep wëll?

(q) Dïd you slëep wéll?

(r) Cän you cöme to téa on Thürsday?

(s) Cän you cöme to tëa on Frίday? (14)

32. *Note what happens when we add something to a sentence or phrase that is already complete in itself. Practise the examples.*

Säy it agàin.   Säy it agàin, plëase.

Göod mòrning.   Göod-mòrning, Mr* Jönes.

It's vëry còld.   It's vëry còld todäy I thïnk.

Plëase sït dòwn.   Plëase sït dòwn, Mrs* Röbinson (6).

I cän't hèar you.   'I cän't hèar you,' she säid (3).

There's nöbody (17) thère.   'There's nöbody thère,' he änswered.

'There's nöbody thère,' said the Träveller, wälking awäy in the snöw (17).

Pitch and Intonation: (2) Rising Tone.

33. (a) (*statement*) One,   two,   three, . . .   (I have not finished)

* Mr: *pronounce* [mìster]; Mrs: *pronounce* [mìsses].

(*b*) (*command*)   Wait!   ✔   (There is more to come)

(*c*) (*question*)   Food?   ✔   (I wonder. Is it true?)

What?   ✔   (I want more information)

Tired?   ✔   (Answer 'Yes' or 'No')

Say the following on a rising tone:

(*a*) four, five, six, seven, eight, nine, ten, . . .
a, b, c, d, e, f, g, h, i, j, k, l, m, n, o, p, q, ..
(*b*) Stand! Look! Turn!
(*c*) Rice? Salt? Wood? Iron?* Yes? No? Who? Whose? When?
Why? How? Where? Right? Wrong? Hot? Cold? Wet? Dry?

34. *Repeat and learn the following, saying each word on a rising intonation except the last. Drop the voice on the last word.*

(*a*) twénty, thírty, fórty, fífty, síxty, séventy, éighty, nínety, | öne hùndred.
(*b*) fírst, sécond (3), thírd, fóurth (7), fífth, síxth, séventh, éighth, nínth (14), ténth, eléventh, twélfth, | thïrtèenth.
(*c*) fóurtëenth, fífteenth, síxteenth, séventeenth, éighteenth, níne-teenth, | twèntieth.
(*d*) twënty-fírst, twenty-sécond, thírtieth, fórtieth, | hùndredth.
(*e*) 1st, 2nd, 3rd, 4th, 5th, 6th, 7th, 8th, 9th, 10th.
(*f*) 21st, 22nd, 23rd, 24th, 25th.
(*g*) Mónday, Túesday, Wédnesday, Thúrsday, Fríday, Sáturday, | Sùnday.
(*h*) Jánuary,† Fébruary,† Márch, Ápril (13), Máy, Júne, Julý, Aúgust (7), Septémber, Octóber (17), Novémber, | Decèmber.
(*i*) Spríng, súmmer, áutumn (7), | wìnter.

Raise your voice on the last word of the group, except at the end:

(*j*) a hündred and óne, a hundred and twó, a hundred and thrée, a hundred and twénty, | twö hùndred.
(*k*) It's öne o'clóck, fïve pást one, tén past, quárter past, twénty past, twenty-fíve past, hálf past, twënty-fïve to twó, twënty tó, quárter to, tén to, fíve to, | twö o'clòck.

* iron (22: *r usually silent*).
† January (4, y + 8, 12, 2). February (*you need not pronounce the first r*).

35. *Practise the following with the intonation indicated:*

Wáter?

Beaútiful?

A bóok?

Some wáter?

In the róom?

In the gárden?

Is it a récord?

Is it Sáturday todäy?

Eighty? Really (18)? Never?

Yesterday? All of it? None of us?

Some tea? Alone? Today?

The doctor? You're going?

Is it true? Has he gone?

In the morning? In the evening?

Was it an accident?

36. *Sentences with more than one stress. Practise:*

Thïrtéen? Last night? Go home?

Thïrty-thrée? Can't you see?

Cän't you ünderstánd? May I have some tea?

Is thät chäir cómfortable?

Ïs this ëxercise dífficult?

37. *Something added to a sentence. Practise:*

Äre you thére?
Mäy I häve some téa?
Is thïs your ráin-cöat?

Äre you thére, Mr Jönes?
Mäy I häve some téa, plëase?
Is thïs your ráin-cöat, Jöhn?

'Is thïs chäir óccupied (6, y + 8, 14)?' 'Is it óccupied?' I äsked.

'Is there änybody thére?' said the Träveller.

'Is there änybody thére?' said the Träveller, knöcking on the möonlit dóor.

34

38. *Use a rising tone at the end of a phrase or clause when it is not the end of a sentence. Practise:*

We gö to wörk in the mòrning.   We gö höme in the èvening.
In the mórning, | we gö to wòrk.   In the évening, | we äll gö hòme.
Ïf it is wét, | we stäy indòors.   We stäy indöors if it is wèt.
Thïs little pïg went to márket, | thïs little pïg stäyed at hòme.
Plëase excùse me. Excüse mě, | cän you tëll me the tíme?

39. *Use a falling-rising tone as a sign of politeness. Practise:*

Normal, plain, abrupt	*Polite, encouraging*
Göod nìght.	Göod nǐght.
Thànk yoü.	Thànk yoú.
Göod mòrning.	Göod mǒrning.
Whät is your nàme?	Whät is your nǎme?
Whät tìme is it?	Whät tǐme is it?
Whät does this mèan?	Whät does this měan?
Whëre is the bùs stöp?	Whëre is the bùs stóp?
Plëase sït dòwn. Dön't gò.	Plëase sït dǒwn. Dön't gǒ.

Pünctuàtion

Füll stòp . Còmma , Quèstion märk ? Hỳphen - Invërted còmmas, " " (or quötation märks). Ëxclamàtion Märk !

40. *Do Exercises 21 and 22 (a to d) as dictation, putting in the* **pünctuàtion märks.**

REVISION

41. (*a*) *Read Exercises 2, 3, 4, 8, 9, 11, 12, 13, 14.*
(*b*) **Count** *from 1 to 20; count in tens from 20 to 100.*
(*c*) *Say* **the days of the week, the months of the year,** *and* **the four seasons.**
(*d*) **Tell the time** *in ïntervals of five minutes from eight o'clock till ten.*
(*e*) **What is the date?** January 16th 1965. (*Say*: Jänuary the sïxtéenth, nïneteen sïxty-fìve). *Say:* February 21st 1642; April 22nd 1770; May 1st 1880; July 8th 1969.

TESTS

42. (*a*) *Arrange the following words in rhyming pairs:* are, bed, break, burn, buy, car, care, come, debt, do, done, dumb, earn, friend, front, get, give, go, good, great, gun, hair, head, near, here, high,

35

hunt, know, live, make, my, not, nought, pleasant, present, run, send, son, sort, there, through, tongue, wait, wear, what, who, why, wood, you, young. [50]

(*b*) *Read correctly:* accept, account, answer, attention, brother, certain, character, comfortable, cover, doubt, exercise, ginger, give, have, hour, house, know, knowledge, laugh, law, listen, man, many, mother, one, only, photograph, photographer, photographic, pleasure, pronounce, pronunciation, right, school, straight, student, study, sugar, through, throw, tomorrow, two, university, walk, want, what, where, who, work, write. [50]

(*c*) *Read Exercise 22, pronouncing the vowels and consonants correctly, and using the intonation indicated.*

Dictation, to test correct hearing and spelling.

(*d*) eat, heat, hit, it, heater; man, men, bed, bad, bird.

(*e*) short, sort, shot, not, nought; head, had, hard, hurt, hut.

(*f*) ear, hear, hair, air, dear; he, see, she, sheet, seat.

(*g*) boat, vote, bush, push, pull; right, long, light, wrist, wrong.

(*h*) the, fee, thing, sink, down; one, two, free, present, pleasant.

(*i*) some, day, summer, soon, runner; ride, writer, lighter, race, lays.

(*j*) three, four, thirteen, forty, eighteen; want, wash, watch, work, walk.

(*k*) Don't shout. Turn left. Write neatly. Where are your friends?

(*l*) What does 'high' mean? How much do these flowers cost?

(*m*) I have only seventy cents. Is that enough? Not quite. [100]

PART TWO

WORDS SERVING DIFFERENT PURPOSES, AND HOW THEY ARE COMBINED

---

2. WORDS REFERRING TO THINGS AND PEOPLE, THEIR KIND, QUALITY AND CONDITION

Nouns and Articles: (1) Màss-Wörds

43. *Learn these* **nouns** *as mass-words:*

earth	rice	cloth	smoke	time
stone	meat	pàper (13)	heat	space
air	salt	ink	light	plèasure
wàter (7)	sugar	glass	sound	pain
life	flesh	wood	music	work
health	blood	mètal (3)	thought (7)	play
grass	skin	iron (22)	feeling	money
corn	bone	steel	knòwledge (6)	love
food	hair	oil	science (22)	peace
bread	wool	fire	art	power [50]

Mass-words, with no article

44.   **Whät is ràin? Räin is wàter.**

Use these patterns to ask and answer questions about: meat, mud, music, science, lèather.

What is bread? Brëad is a kïnd of fòod.

Use these patterns to ask and answer questions about: rice, gold, còtton, milk, silk, sìlver, wheat, soup (9), màrble, elëctric lìght. [15]

45.   **Cöal is blàck. Snöw is whìte.**

Complete: (a) Ice is cold, — is hot. (b) — is green, — — red, — — blue. (c) — — brown, — — yellow. (d) — — hard, — — soft.

Use the same pattern with: (e) wet, dry. (f) hèavy (3), light. (g) sweet, bitter. (h) rough, smooth. (i) sòlid (6), lìquid (2). (j) cheap, expènsive. [20]

37

46. (a) **Whät is ìron lïke? Ïron is hárd and hèavy.**
      Whät cölour is sùgar? Sügar is whíte or bròwn.

Ask and then answer one of these questions about: paper, ink, tea, còffee, coal, ash, smoke, steam, soap, sand. [10]

(b) **Lead (3) is heavy. Whät èlse is hëavy? Ïron is älso hëavy.**

Use these patterns with: white, grey (13), red, yèllow, brown, hard, soft, cold, ùseful, nècessary (3). [10]

47.   **We ëat fòod. We can sëe light.**

Complete: (a) Söme pëople ëat brèad; öther people ëat — . (b) Söme drïnk —, öthers — —. (c) Some — wear —, others — —. (d) — like —, others — —. (e) We all want — and —. (f) We can see —. (g) We can hear —. (h) We — feel —, touch (10) —, taste (13) — and smell —. (i) We can cut —, break —, mëasure —, weigh (13) —, count —, and wrap — in —. (j) We wash with s— and w—. [30]

48.   **Whät is thìs? Pàper. This is pàper. It is pàper.**
              What is that? Ïnk. That is ìnk. It is ìnk.

Repeat each of these patterns 10 times, but use a different word from Exercise 43 every time. Choose words referring to things you can see, feel, taste or smell.

49.   **Thïs tëa is hòt. This is höt tèa. It's höt tèa.**
              That soup is cold. That is cold soup. It's cold soup.

Hot, cold, *etc. are* **adjectives.** *Make a list of all the adjectives in 45 and 46, and add:* good, bad; clean, dirty; new, old; fresh, stale; long, short; thick, thin; warm, cool; strong, weak; bèautiful; ìnteresting; nàtural (4), ärtifìcial (2; *ci* = *sh*). *Then use one of the patterns at the head of this exercise, and a different adjective every time, with 20 nouns from Exercises 43 to 46.*

50.   **Thïs is hòt mïlk; thät is còld mïlk.**

Make up 10 sentences on this pattern using different mass-words and making a contrast between the two adjectives every time.

51.   **This is nöt sált, it ịs sùgar.**

Form 10 sentences on this pattern, making a contrast between the two nouns every time.

Mass-words with some

52. **Plëase gïve me some wàter. Hère is some wäter. Hère is söme.**
Repeat these patterns with 10 different mass-words.

Nouns and Articles: (2) Unit-Words

53. *Learn these nouns as unit-words:*

pèrson	hat	knife	plant	mark
man	coat	fork	tree	sign*
wòman (8)	dress	spoon	branch	point
boy	shoe (9)	cup	leaf	line
girl	house	glass	vègetable	sùrface
fàmily	gàrden	plate	flower	curve
fàther	wall	coùntry (10)	ànimal (4)	àngle
mòther	room	rìver (2)	bird	square
bròther	door	hill	ìnsect	cìrcle
sìster	wìndow	mòuntain	pìcture*	nùmber
bòdy (6)	chair	field (1)	book	wheel
face	table	ìsland*	page	ball
head	desk	town	word	box
eye (14)	bed	shop	name	stick
ear	watch	òffice (6 + 2)	mìnute*	part
hand	clock	school	hour	mèmber
arm	pen	tool	day	side
leg	pencil	hàmmer	week	slope
foot	key (1)	machìne*	month	edge
step	lock	car	year	end

[100]

Unit-words with a (indèfinite àrticle).

54.

Whät is thìs? {
- **A lïne.** Thät is a lïne.
- **An angle.** That is an angle.
- **A circle.** Thät is a pёrfect cìrcle.
}

Repeat with: chair, desk, watch (6), match (4), egg, apple, òrange, step, square, curve, sträight lìne, bёnt stìck, bröken glàss, ёmpty bòttle, old hàt, new dress, clean shirt, dïrty plàte, little bird, dead fly. [20]

* ìsland (14: s *silent*); machìne (*see* 20, *Exceptions*); pìcture: *pronounce* -ture *as* [cher]; mìnute (2, 2,); sign (14; g *silent*).

39

55. Whät is

a màn?	A män is a pèrson.
a bròther?	A bröther is a mëmber of a fàmily.
a mònth?	A mönth is a pärt of a yèar.
a hàt?	A hät is an ärticle of clòthing (17).
a dèsk?	A dësk is an ärticle of fùrniture.*
an àpple?	An apple is a kind of fruit.

Ask the question, and answer it with one of these patterns, about the following, using words from 53: ant, banàna (5), bee, branch, car, càrpet, chàpter, cow, dog, dress, fìnger (ng + g), fly, glove (10), hammer, horse, leaf, minute, potàto (13), room, root, rose, thumb, shirt, wall, wheel. [25]

56. **Whät shäpe is a whèel? A whëel is ròund. Whät èlse is röund?**

(*See Ex.* 46) *Give 5 different answers to the second question.*

Draw: a long line; a tall tree; a short, fat man; a tall, thin man; a thick wall; a square house; a low chair and a high table; a narrow window; a wide door; a mountain with a flat top.

57. **A knìfe has a shärp èdge.**

Use this pattern to answer the following questions: (*a*) What has a flat surface? (*b*) What else has a flat surface? (*c*) What has a sharp point? (*d*) What else? (*e*) What has a high top? (*f*) a tall trunk. (*g*) a long tail. (*h*) a soft wing. (*i*) a steep slope. (*j*) a round handle. *Use the same pattern to say something about:* (*k*) a needle. (*l*) a ràzor (13). (*m*) a cat. (*n*) an old tree. (*o*) a broom. [15]

58. **Ï häve a bròther. I am a stùdent. I wänt to bë a dòctor.**

Make up 10 sentences using the above patterns and the following words: sìster, fàther, mòther, son, dàughter (7), uncle, aunt (5), nèphew, niece (1), gràndfäther, gràndmöther, làwyer, ënginèer, scìentist, wrìter, àrtist, tèacher, àrchitect, fàmous (13) màn, göod frìend.

59   **We gó, cóme, or móve sömething, TÒ a pläce.**
     We stäy ÁT or ÌN a pläce.
     We pùt something ÖN a súrface, but ÏN a spàce.
     We dö something WÏTH an ìnstrument.
     We cùt brëad with a knìfe. We ëat with a knìfe and fòrk.

* Furniture: *pronounce* -ture *as* [cher], *as in* picture.

To, at, in, on, with *are* **prëposìtions**
Complete: (*a*) I write with — —. (*b*) We can write with — — or
— —. (*c*) We put food on — —. (*d*) We keep milk — — bottle.
(*e*) We boil water — — kettle. (*f*) We make tea — — pot. (*g*) We
drink from — — or — —. We buy (14) food at — —. (*i*) We work
at — — or —. (*j*) We sit on — — but sleep in — —. (*k*) We
live in — —. [15]

60. **A. I wänt a pèncil. B. Thère is a pëncil | över thère.**

Repeat with: knife, fork, spoon; cup, sàucer (7), plate, glass;
brush, comb; ènvelope, stamp; match; watch; àpple, òrange; hànd-
kerchief, nèedle, bùtton; nail, screw. [20]

   B. But you hàve* a pëncil: there is a pëncil in your pòcket.
   A. It's äll rìght. I hàve* a pëncil: there is a pëncil on my dèsk.

Use one of these patterns with: fork in your hand; spoon by your
plate; plate under my sàucer; chair in your room; little table by my
bed; watch on your wrist; apple in my bag; handkerchief in my
pocket; water (*see Ex.* 52) in your glass; sugar in your tea; milk in
my coffee; tèlephone (3) in my office; ink in your pen; needle in your
coat; paper in your drawer (20). [15]

a piece of bread, a drop of water.

61.

This is	a pïece (1) of brèad (sòlid)
	a bit of bread
	a loaf (of bread)
	a drop of water (lìquid)
That is	———
Here is	a slice of bread (a pïece cüt flàt)
There is	a ball of string
Get me	a bar of chòcolate (6)
Give me	a blade of grass
Show me	a block of ice
Bring me	a grain of rice
	a heap of earth
	a lump of coal
	a roll of cloth
	a sheet of paper
	a stick of chalk
	a strip of cloth (a löng, thìn pïece)

Draw a slice, ball, bar, block, blade, grain, heap, lump, sheet, stick,
strip. *Learn the phrases in the right-hand column at the head of this*

* *Or, informally,* you've got a pencil, I've got, *etc.*

41

exercise. Form complete sentences using one phrase from the left-hand column and one from the right. Then form complete sentences on the same pattern using the following words: cake, corn, dust, fruit, glass, ink, iron, land, meat, milk, oil, rubber, salt, skin, soap, snow, stone, wheat, wood, wool. [20] *Use* piece *and* bit *once only.*

62.   **A cüp of còffee. A bag of flour. A pound of butter.**

Contàiner	Mèasure	Lìquid	Sòlid
glass, pot,	pound	water, milk,	meat, fruit,
bottle, bowl (17),	ton	tea, wine,	sugar, fat,
bàsin (13), bùcket,	pint (14)	beer, soup,	corn, coal,
kettle, bag,	gàllon	oil, ink,	cheese,
sack, box, tin		paint	chalk (7)
(*or* can)			

Using these words, form 20 phrases on the pattern given at the head of this exercise.

63.   **I wänt a pïece of pàper. Hère is a pïece.**

Repeat these patterns 20 times, using different words from Exercise 61 instead of piece *and* paper.

64.   **a stamp, one stamp**

   A. **Plëase gïve me a stàmp. B. Hère is öne.**
   A. **I want önly *òne* stämp—there are *twò* hére.**
      Hère are twö stàmps.
      ***Öne* stämp is úsed (*zd*) and *öne* is tòrn.**

Repeat with 10 different unit-words instead of stamp, *and with suitable adjectives.*

Nouns used as mass-words or unit-words

65.   **Söund trävels (4) at 365 yärds a sècond.**
      Be quiet. Don't make a sound.
      Nöise is a nùisance (y + 9). Don't make such a noise.
      Metal is heavy. Iron is a metal (i.e. a kind of metal).
      Stöne is a härd sùbstance. There is a stöne in my shòe.

Fill each gap with a mass-word without a, *or a unit-word with* a *or* an, *using one of the following words:* life, light, fire, time, space, food, fuel, pleasure, pain.

   (*a*) — travels faster than sound. There is — by my bed.
   (*b*) We have — in our house in winter. Take care: danger* of —.

* danger: *pronounce* [dane-jer].

42

(c) — is èndless. There is — for work and — for play.
(d) Men can now travel through —. A room is — in a house.
(e) We like — and fear —. I have — in my stòmach.
(f) You have — ïnteresting —. Yes, but — is sömetimes very hard.
(g) We burn —. Coal is — .Oil is —: it is also —.
(h) Good-bye. It was — to see you. [20]

66. *Fill each gap with a mass-word alone, with* some + *a mass-word,
with* piece of —, *or with* a + *unit-word, using one of the following
words:* glass, cloth, iron, paper, money, work, play, job, game,
ïnformàtion, advìce, prògress, fùrniture.

(a) Write your name on a —. We can burn —: we cannot burn
stone. I want to make a fire: bring me —. I want to see the news:
bring me —.
(b) We can see through —. Waiter! There's a — in my soup. Bring
me — of milk instèad.
(c) An iron bar is a long, flat —. We press clothes with —.
(d) We make clothes from —. A handkerchief is a —. We are
going to have dinner: put — on the table.
(e) Can you lend me — please? — is made of metal or paper.
(f) I've fïnished (2) my wòrk: let's have — of tènnis. I wörk in a
fàctory: I have a very interesting —. — is üsually* harder than —.
(g) I wänt to knòw sömething. Can you give me —? That is an
interesting —.
(h) You need help. Let me give you —. This is a useful —.
(i) This room looks empty: it needs —. A chair is a —.
(j) Very good. You are making —. [25]

Unit-words: Singular and Plural

67. *Learn this SCHEME FOR THE PLURAL OF NOUNS:*

	Singular†	Plùral (8)	
(a) *Words ending in vowel or soft consonant*	tree, boy, girl pen, pencil	trees, boys, girls pens, pencils	} *s soft*
(b) *Ending in hard consonant*	cup, hat, book	cups, hats, books	*s hard*
(c) *Ending in hissing sound*	piece, rose, vìllage, dress, match, box	pìeces, ròses, vìllages, drèsses, màtches, bòxes	*extra syllable (iz)*

* usually: *pronounce the* s *as* z *or* [3].
† *Pronounce* 2, y + 8, 12; *and sound the* g *after the* ng, *as in* single.

43

Note that the words in (c) *have an extra syllable in the plural. This happens after a hissing sound—s, z, j, ch, x.*

68. *Learn these exceptions to the scheme in 67:*

Singular	Plural
(*a*) house (*ending in sound* s), bath, path, mouth (*hard th*)	houses (*ending in z + iz*), baths, paths, mouths (*soft th + z*)

(*In the above words the exception is in the pronunciation only.*)

(*b*) bàby (13), coùntry, làdy (13) *and all other words ending in* y *when the letter before the* y *is a consonant.*	bàbies, coùntries, làdies (*In these words, the exception is in the spelling only.*)
(*c*) hèro (18), potàto (13), tomàto (5 *or* 13) *and other words ending in* o, *but not certain words borrowed from other languages, or abbreviations,* e.g. piànos (4), dỳnamos (14), phòtos (17).	hèroes, potàtoes, tomàtoes. (*In these words, the exception is in the spelling only.*)
(*d*) leaf, thief (1), self, shelf, half, calf, wolf (8), knife, life, wife, loaf.	leaves, thieves, selves, shelves, halves, calves, wolves, knives, lives, wives, loaves. *Pronounce all these words with one syllable each, ending in -vz.*

(*In the above, the exception is in both pronunciation and spelling.*)

(*e*) man, gèntleman, wòrkman, *etc.* wòman (8 + 12), child (14), foot (8), tooth (9), mouse, goose (9, s), sheep.	men, gèntlemen, wòrkmen, *etc.* wòmen (2 + 2), chìldren (2), feet, teeth, mice, geese, sheep. (*These are old forms, still used*).
(*f*) pèrson	pèrsons (*sèparate*), pèople (*togèther*)
fish	fìshes (*sèparate*), fish (*togèther*)
pènny	pènnies (*sèparate*), pence (*togèther*)

(*g*) *Use* clothes, tròusers, scìssors *only in the plural, and say* Clothes are . . . *etc.* News *is plural in form, but treat it as singular and say* News is . . . *The same applies to* mäthemätics *and* phỳsics (2). Lens *is singular: the plural is* lenses, *as in 67. Treat* polïce (1) *as plural and say* The police are . . .

69. *Say and then write the plural of:*

person; man, woman and child; lady and gentleman; hüsband and wife; boy and girl; eye and ear; mouth, tooth and lip; knee and foot; niece and nephew; shoe and stocking; hat and coat; house and garden; tree, leaf, branch; sheep and goat; dog and wolf; rat and mouse; fox and goose; loaf and fish; day, week, month; country, city, village, place; church, box, penny; hero; knife and fork; photo, lens; half, life; pocket, handkerchief; library (14), shelf; key. [60]

Unit-words, plural, with no article

70.   **Birds fly. Books are made of paper. I like apples.**

Fill the gaps with unit-words in the plural: (*a*) — walk. (*b*) — swim. (*c*) — eat grass. (*d*) — drink milk. (*e*) — like bones. (*f*) — are made of wood. (*g*) — are made of glass. (*h*) — are made of steel. (*i*) — are made of cotton. (*j*) — are made of leather. (*k*) Men wear — and —, women wear —. (*l*) We keep wine in —. (*m*) We put food on —. (*n*) Some people work in —, others work in —. (*o*) In geömetry (6) we study — and —. (*p*) In mäthemätics, we study —. [20]

71.   **Whät are thèse? Lìnes. Thöse are lìnes. They are lìnes.**

On this model do Ex. 54 in the plural. The adjectives, perfect, etc., remain unchanged.

Wë are stùdents. We wänt to be dòctors.

Repeat these sentences 10 times, replacing doctors *by the plural of words in Ex. 58, adding* sóldiers,* sáilors, *and* aìrmen.

72.   Unit-words, plural, with some

    A. **Plëase gïve me some (12) stàmps.**
    B. **I hàven't any stämps.**
    C. **There are some stämps in that tìn.**
    D. **Hëre you áre. Nòw you häve söme (10).**

Repeat with 10 different unit-words instead of stamps *and* tin.

Unit-words with the (dëfinite àrticle)

73.   **Hëre are twö hàts. Öne is míne, öne is yòurs.**
    Whïch one is yòurs? Thìs öne—the òld öne.

    * soldier: *pronounce* sòld-jer.

Which one is mine? That one—the new one.
The öld hat is yóurs, the nëw hat is mìne.

Repeat with 10 different unit-words instead of hat *and with suitable adjectives.*

74. Here are twö different thìngs. A whïte cóat and a bläck umbrèlla. Whïch is yòurs? The umbrèlla—the bläck umbrèlla?

Repeat with 6 different pairs of words instead of coat *and* umbrella, *and with suitable adjectives.*

75. Hère is a kéy: thère is a lòck. Püt the këy in the lòck.

Repeat 20 times: each time choose one word from the left-hand column and one from the right:

book, pen, letter, pòstcard (17), match, screw, picture, film, cake, button, dress, sùitcase (9), car, egg, apple, flower, plant, bird, spoon, coin.	ènvelope, lètterbox, lìbrary (14), drawer, càmera (4), hole, frame, box, cùpboard,* car, òven (10), bùttonhole, bowl, bàsket, vase,* garage,* nest, saucer, garden, purse. [20]

76. Whère is the kèy? Whïch òne? The këy in Ëxercise 75. Thät key is nöw in the lòck. It is ïn the lòck. Thère is the këy. Thère it ïs.

Repeat with the other 40 words in Ex. 75.

77. Where is the sun? It's in the sky.

Repeat with: moon, sky; sea, world; world, ùniverse (y + 9).

78. Hère is a ròom. Thïs is the dóor, the wíndow, the flóor, the céiling (1), the lìght.

Repeat with: (*a*) hòuse; kítchen, díning-room, bédroom, báthroom, róof, gárden, gáte, ròad. (*b*) tòwn; márket, bánk, póst (17)-öffice, théatre,† stàtion (13). (*c*) plànt; róot, stèm. (*d*) trèe; róot, trùnk. (*e*) bòx; tóp, bóttom, báck, frónt, míddle, léft sïde, rìght sïde.

79. I cän't fïnd (14) the dòor. Thère is the döor. Thère it ïs.

Repeat with: handle, light, switch, kitchen, dìning-room, bàthroom, làvatory (4), lift, wäy ìn, wäy òut, bùs stöp, pòst-öffice, stàtion, bank, polìce-stätion.

* cùpboard (10 + 12: *p silent*); vase (5, *or* 13); gàrage (4 + 5) *or* garàge (12 + 5)—*in either case, pronounce the second g as* [3].
† thèatre: *pronounce* [thèer-ter], hard *th*.

80.　(*a*) Here are twö réd böoks | and twö grèen böoks. The rëd books are mìne. *Complete:* — — — — yours.

(*b*) Hëre are some rëd péncils | and some bläck pèns. The pëns are yòurs. *Complete:* — — — —.

(*c*) Hëre are some létters: thëre are some ènvelopes. Püt the lëtters in the ènvelopes.

Repeat with: matches, pictures, dresses, flowers, suitcases *instead of* letters, *and find suitable substitutes for* envelopes.

(*d*) Where are the lettérs? Which ones? The letters in 80(c). Those letters are in the envelopes. They are in — —. There are the letters. There they are.

Repeat with: matches, pictures, etc.

81.　　　**Here is a face. Here are the eyes and the ears.**

Repeat with: (*a*) mouth, lips, teeth; (*b*) body, shóulders (17), arms, hands, fingers, legs, feet; (*c*) house, walls, windows; (*d*) town, streets, shops; (*e*) country, mountains, rivers, fòrests (6).

Unit-words without an article.

82.　*Learn:*

(*a*)　　See Ex. 78.　　　　　*Idiomatic Expressions.*

Go {	to the door.	Go {	to bed.	Stay {	in bed.
	to the bank.		to school.		in school. (*or* at)
	to the station.		to church.		in church.
	to the post-office.		to hòspital.		in hospital.
	to the theatre.		to prìson (2).		in prison.
	to the shops.		home.		at home.

(*b*) We travel by bícycle (14), by bus, by car, by train, by boat, by ship or by áeroplane (19) (*or* by plane); or we go on foot.

(*c*) I like lemon in my tea—but not a whole lemon, please.

Mass-words with the definite article.

83.　　　**Wäter can be bóiling or nòt boiling.**
　　　　The wäter in this säucepan (7) is bòiling.
　　　　Whàt water is böiling? The wäter in that sàucepan.

Repeat this sequence with the following words, filling in the gaps: water, hot, —, pipe; earth, wet, —, pot; ink, clean, —, —; fruit, —, not ripe, —; ïnformätion, ínteresting, ùnïnteresting, — ; —, —, ùn-

47

hëalthy, tünnel; —, good, —, rëstaurant; light, too strong, too —, —; fürniture, —, expènsive, —; work, hard, èasy, —. [10]

84. **We are häving a mèal. There is some brèad on the table. Päss the brèad, plëase.**

Repeat with: bùtter, salt, pèpper, sùgar, milk, fruit, jam, màrmalade, sauce (7), vìnegar (2).

85. **The water in these saucepans is boiling.**

Repeat Ex. 83 putting saucepan, pipe, pot, etc. into the plural.

Descriptive Adjectives

86. **A nïce pèrson. A bräve màn. A beaütiful wòman.**

Supply an adjective for each of the words in Ex. 53, choosing one of the words below. Say a *(or an)* — —. *Then use each of the words below with a suitable unit-word (with* a*) or mass-word (without* a*):*

(a) *What is your imprèssion of the person or thing?* good/bad; nice/nàsty; pléasant (3)/ùnplëasant*; prétty (2), beaútiful/ùgly; big, great/little.

(b) *mèasurement:* large/small; long/short; wide/nàrrow; thick/thin; fat/thin; high/low; tall/short; deep/shàllow; héavy/light; young (10)/old; fast/slow; éven (*number*)/odd (*number*); expénsive/cheap; rich/poor.

(c) *shape:* straight/bent; cròoked,* curved*; square/round; flat/sloping, steep; sharp/blunt; even/uneven.

(d) *còlour:* dark/light; black/white; red/green.

(e) *fèeling:* hard/soft; dry/wet; hot, warm/cool, cold; smooth/rough; tight/loose*; (*hearing*) loud/soft (e.g. a loud noise).

(f) *taste:* good/bad; sweet/sour, bìtter.

(g) *quàlity:* good/bad; real, nátural/ärtifìcial, unnatural; true/untrue, false; hard, dífficult/èasy; ínteresting/ùnínteresting.

(h) *condìtion:* good/bad; new/old; clean/dìrty; full/èmpty; whole, pérfect/bròken, torn; fresh/stale; strong/weak, hèlpless (*person*); safe/unsafe; happy/sad; héalthy/ùnhëalthy; quiet/noisy; tídy/ùntïdy.

(i) *behàviour* (13): good/bad, nàughty (7); kind/unkind, cruel; gentle/rough; políte/rude; quiet/noisy; cáreful/càreless; tidy/untidy; cléver/stùpid (y + 8); thoughtful/thoughtless; helpful/unhelpful.

* *Pronunciation:* an ünplëasant vòice, *but* Thïs is not pléasant, it's ùnplëasant; crooked: *two syllables* [crook-id]; curved: *one syllable* [curvd] (*see Table* 26); loose (9 + *hard s*).

48

87.   *Nouns*   *Adjectives*
        dirt, mud, stone   **dìrty, mùddy,*** stòny***

The adjective dirty *is formed by adding a süffix to the noun.*
Spell the adjectives formed from bone, dust, flower, fun, hair, health,
hill, ice, leaf, oil, noise, rain, salt, sand, skin, sleep, soap, sun, wind,
wool.* *Use 10 of these adjectives as in 86.*

88. *Learn:*

Nouns	*Adjectives*
fool; beaùty	fòolish; beaùtiful*
care, help, pain, thought	careful, helpful, etc.
	careless, helpless, etc.
father, mother, friend	fatherly, motherly, etc.
dànger, pòison, mòuntain	dàngerous, pòisonous, etc.
rèason; sense	rèasonable; sènsible*
mùsic; science (22)	mùsical; scïentìfic (22, 2, 2)

Adjectives	*Nouns*
(*a*) good, kind, sweet,	gòodness, kìndness, swèetness,
càreful, càreless	càrefulness, càrelessness
(*b*) warm, true, strong,	warmth, truth (9), strength,
long, deep, wide, high	length, depth, width, height (14)
Examples: a true story.	Tell me the truth.

89.   **Thïs is a blàck tïe. I wänt a whìte öne.**

Repeat 40 times to make a contrast with each of the following:
a bad egg, a big box, a blunt needle, a cheap prësent, a crooked stick,
a dark room, a dirty cloth, an expensive seat, a full bottle, a hard
cushion, a hard question, a heavy süitcase, a high stool, a hot drink,
a light colour, a light weight (13), a loose cöllar, a noisy hotël, an
odd number, an old rëcord, an old horse, a rough surface, a rough
manner, a rude waiter, a sad story, a short chain, a short man, a slow
train, a soft bed, a soft voice, a stale loaf, a stùpid boy, a thin face, a

* *Important Spelling Instructions*
   1. *Whenever a stressed syllable (e.g.* rùn, begìn) *ends in a single consonant letter*
preceded by a single vowel letter, double the final consonant before an ending that
begins with a vowel letter (e.g. rùn, rùnning, rùnner; stop, stopped; begìn, begìnning,
begìnner). *However, woolly may have double* l *in spite of the two o's.*
   2. *When a word ends in mute* e (e.g. come), *omit the* e *before an ending that*
begins with a vowel sound (e.g. come, coming).
   3. *When a word ends in* y *preceded by a consonant, change the* y *to* i *before any*
*ending (*beauty, beautiful) *except an ending beginning with* i *itself (*try, trying).

thin blänket, a tight knot, an ugly view, a warm shirt, a wet towel (16), a wide belt, the wrong answer. [40]

Adjuncts

90. **Thïs is a wàll. It is mäde of stòne. It's a stöne wàll.**

On the same pattern, make 40 combinations from the following:

What is it?	What is it made of?
bag, ball, band, belt, box, brick, building, can, coin, fence, jèrsey, pie (14), rail, ring, rod, sàlad (4), sheet, shirt, wall, watch	apple, brick, cemènt, copper, cotton, fruit, gold, iron, leather, metal, mud, paper, rubber, silk, silver, steel, tin, wire, wood,* wool*

91. **The wïndow in my bédroom | is my bëdroom wìndow.**
     The döor to the kítchen | is the kïtchen dòor.
     A chäir üsed in a díning-room | is a dïning-room chàir.

Answer on the same pattern:

What is a cärpet for a dràwing-room; the desk in my office; the gate to your garden; a doctor in a village; the clock at the station; the hall in our school; the walls round the city; an exäminätion in a ünivèrsity; an offïcial† in a gòvernment (10); a road over a mountain; an evening in winter; a mörning in Octòber (17)?

Compound Nouns

92. **(a) Whät kïnd of shïp is thàt? It's a spàce shïp.**
     (b) Whät kïnd of brùsh is thät? It's a tòoth-brush.
     (c) Whät kïnd of knìfe is thät? It's a pènknife.
     (d) Whät is a störy abòut lòve cälled? A lòve-störy.
     (e) Whät is a böx for màtches cälled? A màtch-box.

Ask and answer questions on this pattern of a, b and c to form:

(*a*) flòwer shöp; shèep färm; alàrm bëll; bùs tïcket; ràilway brïdge; gòld mïne; quèstion märk; tràde märk; dànger sïgn; fìre stätion.

(*b*) tèa-cup; ègg-cup; soùp-plate; tèa-pot; frùit-tree; ràin-coat; hànd-bag; màtch-box; hàir-oil; fàce-pöwder; tòoth-paste (13); stòre-room; rìght-ängle; wàsh-bäsin; dòor-bell; hànd-brake; fòot-

---

* *Use the adjectives* wöoden *and* wöollen *in the third sentence.*
† offïcial (2: *ci = sh*).

pump; light-bulb; pìcture-frame; fìnger-nail; fìnger-mark; pòcket-book; sèa-water; sìlk-worm. *Note:* ärm-chàir.

(*c*) fòotball; snòwball; bàthroom; bèdroom; hairpin; sùnlight; mòonlight; fìrewood; dùstpan; blàckboard; bòokcase.

Now ask and answer questions on the pattern of (d) and (e) about:

(*d*) a lesson about science; a book about physics*; a field for football.

(*e*) a book for notes; a brush for teeth; a box for tools; a bowl for fingers; a peg for clothes*; a basket for eggs; juice from lemons; a shop for newspapers; leather for shoes.

93. **Whät is the wàter† lìke? Ìcy.**
     Whät kìnd of bòx is thät? An ìce-box.

In the following sentences, fill the gaps with either an adjective formed from the noun in brackets, or with an adjunct:

(*a*) (sun) In — weather, I wear — glasses.
(*b*) (rain) In — weather, I wear a — coat.
(*c*) (wind) On a — day, we can measure the force of the wind by a — instrument.
(*d*) (soap) Soap is made in a — factory. Don't drink — water.
(*e*) (sand, stone) Vegetables grow in — soil but not in — ground.
(*f*) (beauty) We see — girls in a — competition.
(*g*) (music) I take — lessons, because I am —.
(*h*) (danger) There is a — sign. We are coming to a — corner.
(*i*) (science) Not all — teachers are —.
(*j*) (poison) This stuff is —. Keep it in a — bottle.

Order of words before a noun. Noun phrases.

94. **The nëw bröwn lëather glöves in the häll are mìne.**
     Whöse is thät bìg bläck Amërican (3) càr at the döor?

The words new, brown, leather, *and* in the hall *all describe the noun* gloves *and help to identify the gloves that are mine. What can we say about* big black *etc.? Put such words in the following order:*

First—a, *or* the, some, this, that, these, those, my, your, *etc.*
Second—*descriptive adjectives; but*—
Third—*put adjectives of colour after others, except*—
Fourth—*adjectives referring to places.*

* *See* 68 (*g*). *Do not put* physics *and* clothes *into a singular form.*
† What water? (*See Ex.* 83.) The water in the swimming pool, for example.

Fifth—Put adjuncts after adjectives and immediately before the noun; and

Sixth—put phrases after the noun.

Arrange the words in brackets below in order according to the models and instructions above, and then read and write out each complete sentence:

(a) This is (sand, yellow, soft). (b) I want (bread, white, fresh, some). (c) Look at (the, sea, blue, deep). (d) Bring me (that, warm, in the basin, water). (e) Where are (my, glasses, sun, black)? (f) Here is (a, wall, stone, low, grey). (g) George is (a, engineer, radio, young). (h) (That, long, in my drawer, envelope) is for you. (i) Sit on (cushion, comfortable, air, this). (j) (The, vase, on the table, Chinese,* green, beautiful) is broken.

Predicate and Attribute

95.   (a) **I wash a cup and put it on the shelf.**
              (b) **The cup is now clean.**
              (c) **The clean cup is on the shelf.**

In sentence (b) we say that 'the cup' *is the* sùbject *of the sentence, and* 'is clean' *the* prèdicate. *We are therefore using the adjective* 'clean' *predicatively. In sentence (c) we say that the cup now has the* quàlity *or* àttribute *of clean-ness, and the adjective* 'clean' *is here used* attrìbutively.

Predicative	*Attributive*
Thïs böx is hèavy.	**Thïs is a hëavy bòx.**
Thïs böx is for ïce.	**Thïs is an ïce-box.**

Using the patterns in the left-hand column, say the following sentences in a different way (see 91 and 92):

(a) This is an interesting story. (b) This is a war story.
(c) This is a Chinese cupboard (d) This is a china cupboard.
(e) This is sweet juice. (f) This is grape juice.
(g) This is a broken bottle. (h) This is a beer bottle.
(i) This is an honest official. (j) This is a government official.

96. *Learn:*

Attributive	*Predicative*
Tom is a healthy boy;	**but he is not well today.**
His father is a sick man.	**He is often sick (or ill).**

* Chìna (14, 12); Chinèse (14, 1).

A lïving (2) crèature.	Is it lïving (or alïve (14))?
The Sleeping Beauty.	She is sléeping (or aslèep).
—	She is not awàke yet.
A closed shop.	The shops are closed (or shut).
An expënsive matèrial (15).	Silk is expensive (or dear).

Avoid using well, ill, alive, asleep, awake *and* shut *attributively. On the other hand, do not use adjuncts predicatively in the same way as adjectives (see 95).*

97. (a)   <u>Adjective without a noun</u>

> Thïs is nöt a rìpe pëach: gïve me a rìpe öne.
> I want the ripe peach: give me the ripe one.
> Thëse are nöt rìpe pëaches: gïve me some rìpe önes.
> I want the ripe peaches: give me the ripe ones.

Repeat all four lines with:
sweet orange, fresh loaf, clean handkerchief, cheap card, sharp knife.

(b) *Note* the living, the dead, the sick, the blind (16), the deaf, the dumb, the poor, the rich, the young, the brave, the old, *meaning* living people in general, living people as a class, *etc. Examples:*

> Speak well of the dead. Take care of the sick.
> Help the blind. Nöne but the bräve desërve the fàir.

A handful

98.   My pöcket is fùll. It's füll of sàndwiches.*
        I have a pöcketful of sàndwiches.

Form sentences on these patterns, using:
handful, armful, mouthful, spoonful, bagful, basketful, bucketful.

Plural of adjunct + noun and of compound nouns

99. *Learn:*

Singular	*Plural*
flower shop, egg-cup	flower shops, egg-cups,
football, handful	footballs, handfuls

Excèptions:

fàther-in-läw, etc.	fàthers-in-läw, etc.
pässer-bỳ	pässers-bỳ

* *Pronounce* sandwich *as* [san-widge].

53

Give the plural of:

apple-tree, rose-garden, fountain-pen, arm-chair, railway, railway station, writing-table, number plate, mother-in-law, brother-in-law, bucketful, book-shelf, tooth-brush, match-box, fig-leaf. [15]

Proper Nouns

100. *Proper Nouns, i.e. names of people and places, do not normally take an article. But note the following exceptions:*

(*a*) (*countries: names formed from a unit-word, e.g. state, union, island*) The Unïted Stätes of Amèrica; The Ünion of Söviet Söcialist Repùblics; The Philippine Islands.

(*b*) (*rivers, seas, mountain ranges, ships, newspapers*) The Rïver Nìle (*or simply*, The Nile); The Red Sea; The Atläntic Òcean (17: ce = sh) (*or simply*, The Atlantic); The Rocky Mountains (*or simply*, The Rockies); The Quëen Elìzabeth; *The Times.*

(*c*) (*family or group of people with the same name*) The Smiths.

(*d*) *Note: we can say:* The Ünivërsity of Óxford, *or* Öxford Ünivèrsity; The äirport at Àthens (4), *or* Äthens Àirport; The rädio station at Cáiro (14), *or* Cäiro Ràdio (Station).

I cöme from Utòpia.* I am Utòpian. My fëllow-coüntrymen are Utòpians. I speak Utopian (or the Utöpian lànguage).

Supply the name of your own country instead of Utopia in the above sentences. Note that when the name of the nationality ends in a hissing sound, we say: My fellow-countrymen are (*for example*) Brìtish, Chinèse, Dànish (13), Ènglish, French, Japanèse, Portuguèse, Singalèse, Spànish (4), or Spàniards, Welsh. *Note:* The Japanese (in general: *see* 97*b*) use the same kind of writing as the Chinese.

TABLE 6
Summary of the Use of the Articles

Exercises Use **no article**—

44–51

(*a*) *with a mass-word, to suggest:* (*i*) *a thing in general;* (*ii*) *an indefinite example of it;* (*iii*) *one thing and not another; e.g.*

(i) Grass is green. (ii) This is grass. (iii) It is grass not corn.

* Utòpia: *pronounce* (y + 8, 17, 18).

70–71   (*b*) *with a unit-word in the plural, to suggest:* (*i*) *the objects in general;* (*ii*) *indefinite examples of them;* (*iii*) *one class of object and not another; e.g.*

(i) Birds fly. (ii) Those are birds. (iii) They are birds, not àeroplanes (19).

82   (*c*) *with a unit-word in the singular;* (*i*) *in conventional expressions, which refer to the general idea of a thing rather than a particular example of it; or* (*ii*) *to suggest the substance of a thing rather than the thing as a whole, e.g.*

(i) We go to school by bus. (ii) I like lemon in my tea.

(*d*) *with names of persons and places, e.g.*
Shàkespeare, Áthens, Austràlia (6, 13, 18)

Use the indefinite article, a

54–60   (*e*) *with a unit-word,* (*i*) *to suggest that an object is an example of a class bearing a certain name; or* (*ii*) *to suggest one indefinite example of a class, e.g.*

This is a book (*emphasis on class*). Give me a book (*one example*).

(*For* one, *see 64; and for* some, *see 52, 72.*)

Use the definite article, the

73, 80a   (*f*) *with a unit-word, as a sign that you are referring to one or more examples of a class and that you assume your hearer knows which example or examples you mean, e.g.*

Here are three books of different sizes: the biggest book is yours, the smaller books are mine.

74, 80b   (*g*) *with a unit-word, as a sign that you are referring to a particular class of thing, and are distinguishing it from another class or other classes, e.g.*
The teacher teaches. The learner learns.

75–79   (*h*) *with a unit-word, as a sign that you are referring to one*
80c, d, 81   *or more known or identifiable members of a class, when you are not concerned with the existence of other members of that class, e.g.*

Go to the door. Open the window.
The sun and the moon are in the sky.

83–85   (*i*) *with a mass-word, in the singular only, as a sign that you are referring to a known or specified part of the mass, e.g.*

Please pass me the bread—I mean the bread on the table.

100   (*j*) *with place names, when they are formed by unit-words or when they specify which sea and which river (see 100b); e.g.*

The United States of America. The Soviet Union. The River Rhine (*or* the Rhine). The Atlantic (Ocean).

100   (*k*) *with names of people, when referring to two or more people of the same name, e.g.*

The Smiths (*i.e.* Mr and Mrs Smith, or the Smith family).

Passages for reading and dictation

101. Our höuse ständs by the sïde of a wïde ròad. It has a smäll gärden in frónt of it | and a lärge gärden behïnd. There are flöwers in the frónt gärden, | and früit-trees and vëgetables at the bàck. In wärm wëather, we häve our mëals öutsïde. Whën it is hót, | the ëarth gëts vëry drỳ. Thén, | in the évening, | we must wäter it with a hòse-pïpe.

The höuse has a flät róof | and whïte wàlls. The frönt döor lëads into a lïttle hàll, | where we häng our häts and còats. On the lëft of the háll | is a dïning-röom, | where we üsually häve our mèals. On the rïght is the dràwing-röom, | where we recëive (1) vísitors, | or réad, | lïsten to the rádio (13), | or wätch the tëlevïsion. Fäther älways türns on the rädio to hëar the nèws. The kïtchen is at the bàck of the höuse.

Üpstáirs | there are thrëe bëdrooms and a bàthroom. From my bëdroom wïndow I can see snöwy mòuntains, | fär awày. Whät a wönderful vïew!

102. We lïve nëar a bïg tòwn. It has some fïne öld bùildings (2) | and mäny nëw cóncrete önes | füll of òffices. Fäther wörks in öne of thëse grëat blòcks. He sïts at a désk, | wrïtes létters | and änswers the tèlephone. I dön't knöw whät èlse he dòes (10).

My bröther häs a jöb in a fàctory. He drïves thère in a sëcond-händ càr. I thïnk it is dàngerous. The tÿres are älmost (7, 17) wörn òut, | and the ëngine is älways gïving troùble (10). He drïves töo fàst. There are töo mäny cärs on the ròads, | töo mäny pëople in the närrow strèets, | and töo müch nòise. Fórtunately, | our schöol büilding is in a quïet ärea (19 + 18) awäy from the tràffic. It has lïght, äiry cláss-röoms, | and a lïbrary (14) with sëveral (3) thöusand bòoks. The schöol ständs on the ëdge of a lärge fìeld (1) | where we pläy gämes twïce a wèek. We have lëssons ëvery (3) däy excëpt Sünday, | and we have thrëe mönths' höliday (6) a yèar.

103. The pëople who lïve nèar us | are our nèighbours (13). The pëople who lïve nëxt dòor to us | are our nëxt dòor nëighbours. Our nëxt döor nëighbours are the Frèemans. Döctor Frëeman is the profèssor of physics at the Ünivèrsity. His wïfe is the pràctical mëmber of the fämily. They have twö sóns, | Jöhn (6) and Geórge, | and twö dàughters, | Jäne and Màry (19). Jöhn is twënty-òne, | and is clèver, quïet and cäreful, lïke his fàther. Geörge is sïxteen | —càreless, | üntïdy, | but vëry amùsing (y + 9). Jáne, | who is nïnetéen, | is prètty, | lïke her mòther. Märy is önly twèlve. She is a räther wèak chïld | and öften ìll, | but ëverybody is fònd of her.

104. A cómpass (10) | is an ïnstrument with a nêedle | that älways pöints in the säme dirèction. The chief diréctions, | or pöints of the cómpass, | are nórth, sóuth, éast and wèst. The sün rïses in the éast in the mörning, | and sëts in the wést in the èvening. At mïd-dăy, we sëe it in the söuth, if we lïve in the nórthern hëmisphere (3, 2, 18), | and in the nörth if we lïve in the soùthern (10) hëmisphere. At nïght, the stàrs appëar (18).

Coüntries (10) in Eürope (y + 9, 12) have a cöld clïmate (14) in wínter, | and a cöol or a wärm clïmate in sùmmer. Öne däy it is fïne and ëven (1) hòt, | the nëxt day it mäy be cöld, wïndy and wèt.

105. A tÿpewriter is a machïne that wrìtes. It has about fïfty kèys (1), öne for ëach lëtter of the älphabet, | öne for ëach nümber from nöught to nïne, | the rëst for dïfferent sïgns and pünctuàtion märks. It has a härd rübber röller at the bàck. To tÿpe a létter, | you put a shëet of päper behïnd the röller, | and türn the röller untïl the töp of the päper cömes betwëen the röller and an ïnky rìbbon. Whën you toüch (10) a këy with your fínger, | it räises a lïttle hàmmer. At the ënd of this hämmer there is the förm of a létter, fígure (2 + 12) or sìgn. The hämmer hïts the ríbbon | and lëaves a märk on the pàper.

TESTS

106. **What is truth? What is a box? What are bees?**
What is the moon?

Use one of these patterns with each of the following, and then answer the question: ants, blood, bottle, branch, brothers, cow, corn, èlephant (3), finger, flour, flower, fruit, glove, grapes, hour, Ìndia, ink, jam, Lòndon, match-box, needle, orange, rain, ràzor, sea, stick, stone, thumb, wheat, world. [30]

107. **Whät beaütiful wèather! Whät a fïne dày!**

Put what *or* what a (an) *before:* good idea, kind man, hard work, interesting story, narrow streets, soft hand, dirty hands, stüpid boy, dängerous thïng to dò, peace! [10]

108. *Put* a, an, the, some, one *or nothing, before the words in brackets:*
   (*a*) We put (water) in (bath), (matches) in (box), and (beer) in (barrels).
   (*b*) (Fire) is red, (ash) is grey. (Smoke) from this (fire) is black.
   (*c*) We put (ash) from (cigarette) in (ash-tray).
   (*d*) (Sheets) are made of (cotton), (blankets) of (wool).
   (*e*) (Car) is (machine). (Carpet) is (article) of (furniture).
   (*f*) I want (loaf) of (bread), (milk) and (biscuits*).
   (*g*) Please go to (post-office) and buy me (stamps).
   (*h*) I must get (new hat). I want (good one).
   (*i*) Here are two (hats). Which one is yours? (brown one).
   (*j*) What (hot day)! All (food) in our (ice-box) is bad.
   (*k*) I go to (school) by (bus) and come (home) on (foot).
   (*l*) At (school) we study (science) and (mathematics).
   (*m*) (Students) study (law) and (medicine) at (university).
   (*n*) Please give me (ink). There is (ink) in (bottle) on that table.
   (*o*) When I write (letter), I put (date) at (top) of (paper).
   (*p*) What (wonderful weather)! There is not (cloud) in (sky).
   (*q*) It's dark in this (room). Turn on (light). I can't find (switch).
   (*r*) Manïla is (cäpital) of (Phìlippine Ïslands).
   (*s*) (river Ganges†) rises in (Himalayas†) and flows into (Bay of Bengàl).
   (*t*) In physics we study (heat), (light) and (sound).
   (*u*) We have quite (good knowledge) of (English). We are making (progress). [70]

* *Pronounce* biscuit *as* [bìskit]. † *Pronounce* [gàn-jees] [hïmmer-làyers].

109. *Put all the nouns (but not the mass-words or adjuncts) into the plural, and make other changes that then become necessary:*

    (a) A city is a big town; a village is a small place.
    (b) On a summer evening, we have a meal in the open air.
    (c) A book-shelf is a long board or sheet of metal.
    (d) A knife is an instrument with a sharp blade.
    (e) Put this match and this leaf in that box.
    (f) Write an answer to the following question.
    (g) In the picture, we see a man, a woman and a child.
    (h) A mother-in-law is the mother of a husband or wife.
    (i) There is a lady and gentleman outside.
    (j) There is a sheep in the field, and a wolf in the forest. [30]

110.   (a) *Give 20 examples of the pattern* a (piece) of (paper), *but do not use the words in brackets.*

    (b) *Give 10 examples of the pattern* a (stöne wàll), *and 10 of the pattern* a (tèa-cup), *but do not use the words in brackets. Then put all the examples into the plural.*

    (c) *Form adjectives from:* sun, rain, noise, beauty, help, friend, danger, reason, music, science; *and nouns from:* good, kind, sweet, warm, true, strong, long, high, wide, deep. [20]

3. IDENTITY, QUANTITY AND DEGREE

Pronouns

111. 'He' *refērs to a person or animal that we think of as a male*—a man, a father, a son, a waiter, an actor, a bull. *The word* 'he' *is* **màsculine** (4, 8, 2). 'She' *refers to a person or animal that we think of as a fèmale* (1, 13)—a woman, a mother, a daughter, a wàitress, an àctress, a cow. *The word* 'she' *is* **fèminine** (3, 2, 2). A child, a friend, a neighbour, *can be male or female.* A child, *etc. therefore can be* 'he' *or* 'she'. 'It' *refers to a thing; or to a person or animal that we do not specially think of | as male or female. The word* 'it' *is* **neùter** (y + 9). 'They' (13) *refers to things, persons or animals in the plural—masculine, feminine or neuter.* He, she, it *and* they *are* **pẽrsonal prònouns.**

Which pronoun would you use in refẽrring to: John, Anne, a tree, an oak, James, Elízabeth, an uncle, an aunt, a húsband, a wife, a flower, a rose, Wílliam, Márgaret, a proféssor, a públisher, an ẽnginéer, notebooks, a teacher, a nephew, a niece, a néwspaper, the Daïly Póst, gloves, an actress, a sécretary, hándkerchiefs, shirts, whïte háir, a wàlking-stïck? [30]

112. *Read the following as dìalogues. Then repeat each dialogue three times, using words from the last exercise instead of those in italics.*

A says:	*B says:*
(*a*) Whät is thàt? Whät ìs it?	It is a *star.* It's* a *star.*
What *star* ìs it?	I don't know its* name.
And what one is that?	Oh, that's *Venus.*
(*b*) Who is that? Who is it?	It's *George* Freeman.
That's his name, but who is he?	He's my *neighbour.*
And what is he?	He's a *student.*
(*c*) *George* Freeman is a *student.*	I can see six *students.* Which is *George* Freeman?
He's the one with *glasses.*	
(*d*) Who's that?	It's *Mary* Baker.
That's her name, but who is she?	She's my *coùsin* (10).
And what is she?	She's a *nurse.*
(*e*) Whose are these five *keys*?	One is yours, three are mine.
Which is my *key*?	This is. Which *keys* are mine?
Those are. And the other one?	
Whose is it?	I don't know whose it is.

* *Notice the difference between* it's (*i.e.* it is) *and its.*

IDENTITY, QUANTITY AND DEGREE

[*Note:* What, which, whose + *noun are interrogative adjectives.*
What, which, whose *alone are interrogative pronouns.*
Who *is only used as a pronoun.*
This, that, these, those *are demonstrative adjectives or
pronouns.*]

113. *Read and repeat the following as a conversation, with three
people, A, B and C:*

A says:	*B says:*	*C says:*
(a) I have a *pencil.*	Ï have öne, | tòo.	Sö have Ì.
(b) But I haven't a *pen.*	Ï haven't öne, | either.*	Nör have Ì.
(c) There's some *note-paper* on the *desk.*	Ïs there äny *note-paper?*	Yès, | there is söme.
(d) But we haven't any *ink.*	Ïs there äny *ink?*	Nò, | there isn't äny.
(e) There are some *envelopes.*	Äre there äny *envelopes?*	Yès, | there àre söme.
(f) But we haven't any *stamps.*	Äre there äny *stamps?*	No, | there àren't äny.
(g) Where's my *pencil?*	It's in your hand.	Yoù häve it.
(h) Where's the *note-paper?*	It's on the *desk.*	Hère it ïs.
(i) Where are the envelopes?	They are in the drawer.	Thère they äre.
(j) Where are the stamps?	We haven't any.	There àren't äny.
(k) Who's that?	Your *father.*	It's your *father.*
(l) Where's my *father?*	Över thère.	He's över thère.
(m) Where's my *mother?*	At home.	She's at home.
(n) Where are your brothers?	At school.	They're at school.
(o) Where are your sisters?	In the garden.	They're in the garden.

*Now use the same patterns with the following words instead of those
in italics:* knife, fork; bread, table, butter; sàusages (6), eggs; cùpboard; uncle, aunt, nèphew, nieces.

* eìther (14 or 1).

61

TABLE 7

Personal Pronouns; Possessive Adjectives and Pronouns

Singular

1st Person	I am		I have my book.		mine.
2nd „	You are	a student.	You have your book.	It is	yours.
3rd „	He is		He has his book.		his.
	She is		She has her book.		hers.

Plural

1st Person	We are		We have our books.		ours.
2nd „	You are	students.	You have your books.	They are	yours.
3rd „	They are		They have their (19) books.		theirs.

114. *Learn Table 7 by heart.*

The Possessive Form

115. **Whose house is this? That's mỳ house. It's mine. It's my òwn (17).**

Repeat with all persons, singular and plural, and with the following words: garden, field, farm, trees, sheep (*plural*); lùggage, handbag, sùitcases, tìckets, car. [10]

116. **Thät cämera belöngs to Jòhn. It's Jòhn's cämera. It's Jòhn's.**
This belongs to my brother. It's my brother's.
These belong to your friends. They are your friends'.
This belongs to James. It is James's.
This belongs to Mr Church. It is Mr Church's.

(*a*) *Use the pattern with apöstrophe* s or s apòstrophe, to express the relation between:* Mr. Rose and his umbrella; your mother and her bìrthday; your sisters and their admirers; the Prësident (3) and his wìfe; the söldiers and their bòots. [5]

(*b*) *Use the same pattern for:* a dog and its tail, a cat and its paw, an elephant and its trunk, a lion (22) and its roar (20), a tïger (14, g) and its spòts. [5]

* *Pronounce* [a|pos|tro|phee], *4 syllables.*

62

117. (a) **I have mäny frìènds. Fränk is òne. He's a frìènd of mïne. Fränk has sëveral coùsins. Hënry is a coüsin of Frànk's.**

Repeat four times, beginning: You have —, Märgaret has —, We have —, Dävid (13) and Joan have —, *and replacing* cousins *by* students, clients (22), pàrtners, ènemies (3).

(b) **Thïs is the wäll buïlt (2) by Hàdrian (13). It's Hädrian's wàll.**

Repeat with: the hat worn by Napòleon (17); the theatre used by Shakespeare; the bïrthday of the Prèsident; the bïrthplace of Dànte (4 + 2); a play about the death of Caèsar.*

(c) **I am going to my brother's, to the baker's.**

Repeat with: my sìster-in-läw, the dòctor, my tàilor, the gròcer (17) the bùtcher (8), Mr and Mrs Tàylor (Mr and Mrs Taylor's).

118. *Read the following as a dialogue. Then cover up the right-hand column, read the sentences on the left, and repeat those on the right from memory:*

A says:	B says:
(a) Thïs is a jöb for a bòy.	That's a bòy's jöb.
(b) These are clothes for a girl.	Those are a gìrl's clöthes.
(c) These are clothes for girls.	Those are gìrls' clöthes.
(d) This is work for a man.	That's a màn's wörk.
(e) This is work for men.	That's mèn's wörk.
(f) These are toys for children.	Those are chìldren's töys.
(g) The place for a woman is at home.	A wöman's pläce is at hòme.
(h) Look at that boy: his coat is torn to pieces.	Thät böy's cöat is törn to pìeces.
(i) This is the office of one of the secretaries.	That's a sècretary's öffice.
(j) This is the office of the secretary.	That's the sècretary's öffice.
(k) These are the offices of the secretaries.	Those are the sècretaries' öffices.
(l) These are the offices of the bànk mänager.	Those are the bànk mänager's öffices.
(m) This is the office of my brother-in-law.	That's your bròther-in-läw's öffice.
(n) That's the daughter of the King of Spain.	That's the Kïng of Späin's dàughter.†

* Caesar = [Sèezer].
† *A reference to an old song, but a useful pattern for modern English.*

63

119. **An hòur's lèsson. A day's peace. Twö wëeks' wòrk.**

Use this pattern to express the length of time taken by: a joùrney (11), a hòliday (6), a walk, thought, silence (14), àbsence, a rest, a drive, sleep, illness.

The relation between the part and the whole

120. **A part of a thing. The back of a chair.**

Use this pattern to express the relation between: the stairs, the top; the sea, the bottom; the table, the middle; the term, the beginning; this month, the end; my house, the side; your tie, the colour; that box, the weight (13); this road, the length; that building, the height (14). [10]

121. **The sïde of the röad is the ròad-sïde.**

Repeat with: side, sea*; side, river; side, mountain; bank, river; top, hill; top, tree; top, roof; end, week*; handle, door; holder, pen.

122. **A man's hand. The hand of a clock. The road-side.**

Use one of these patterns to express the relation between: my wife and her relàtions; Thomas and his addrèss; this table and its legs; a mountain and its top; the wall and its colour; a cow and its horns; a pärcel and its wèight; a child and its pàrents (19); a speaker and his sùbject; a book and its tìtle (14). [10]

other, same, next, only

123. *Read, filling the gaps:*

(*a*) Write down a number. Write down another number. Now another one; and another; and one more.

(*b*) Here are five numbers: 16, 18, 23, 41, 16.

(*c*) The first number is —, the second is —, the third — —, the fourth — —, the fifth — — again.

(*d*) The first is —, the next number is —, the next — —, the next — —, the last — —. The first is the same as the —.

(*e*) The — and the — are the same. The other numbers are different. The third is not — — — — —.

(*f*) The second is 18. The third is not the — number, it is a — one.

(*g*) The — is the only number over 25: — is the only one over 25. The — and the — are the only numbers under 18. There is only one number — —. There are only two numbers — —.

* See note.

Use other, same *and* next *as adjectives and pronouns.* Use *only as an adjective, not as a pronoun. If a noun is omitted, say* the only one.

124.

Adjective	Pronoun
another number, another one	another
other numbers, other ones	others
the other number, the other one	the other
the other numbers, the other ones	the others

Form 7 sentences using another, other *and* the other *as adjectives, then* another, others, the other, the others *as pronouns.*

125. *Learn Table 8.*

TABLE 8

WHOLE and PART

Höw müch of a màss? Whät **amòunt**?

The whòle amöunt	—ALL
Part: a cèrtain amöunt; not all, not none	—SOME
: an ùncertain amöunt	—ANY
Nò amöunt	—NO, NONE*

Höw mäny ùnits? Whät **nùmber**?

		More than two	Two only
1 1 1 1 1 1 1	—The whòle nümber	—ALL	BOTH
1 1 1 1 1 1 1	—The sëparate ünits, äll pòsitive	—EVERY*	EACH
|1|1|1|1|1|1|1|	—The units, one by one	—EACH	
1	—A certain one	—ONE	ONE
1 1 1 1	—A certain (plural) number	—SOME	
???????	—An uncertain one or number, chosen from all	—ANY	EITHER*
XXXXXXX	—Every öne nègative	—NOT ANY	NOT EITHER
————	—The whole number negative	—NO, NONE	NEITHER*

* *Use* no *and* ëvery (3) *as adjectives only. Use* none, ëvery òne, ëach òne, *as pronouns. Use all the other words in this table as both adjectives and pronouns. Pronounce* ëither *and* nëither *with vowel 14 or 1.*

---

126. *Suppose the seven units in Table 8 are cards with numbers, 1 to 7. Practise and learn the following dialogue:*

A says:	*B says:*
(*a*) I have all the cards.	I have no cards, I have none.
(*b*) I have every card—1, 2, 3, 4, 5, 6 and 7.	I haven't any—1, 2, 3, 4, 5, 6, or 7.
(*c*) I put each card on the table, one by one. Count.	One; two; three; four; five; six; seven.
(*d*) I give three or four cards to you. Don't look. How many have you?	Three or four. I don't know exactly how many.
(*e*) I still have some cards. I don't know how many, either. But have I a fixed number?	Of course you have.
(*f*) In any case, I have some. Have you some cards too?	Yes, I have some too.
(*g*) Are any of the cards on the floor—1, 2, 3, 4, 5, 6 or 7?	Not one. Every card is on the table.
(*h*) Now take two cards, 1 and 2. Where are the two cards?	Both are in my right hand.
(*i*) Put one card in each hand.	I have one in each hand.
(*j*) Is either of the cards on the table, either 1 or 2?	No, neither of the cards is on the table, neither 1 nor 2.

127. *Study Table 8 again. Then read and study the following examples:*

A. How much of a mass?

(i) ALL water is wet, but not all water is fresh. All the water in this tank—all of the water in it—is fresh. All of it. It is all fresh.

(ii) ANY water is wëlcome (3, 12) to a very thirsty man. Have you any milk? I'm sörry (6) we haven't any. But any of the wine here is good—drink what you want. Thank you, but I don't want any of it.

(iii) SOME water is salty—not all. Will you have some water? Thank you, I have some. Some of the milk in the ice-box is sour. Some of it is still fresh.

(iv) These flowers have no water—they must have some. Now they have none.

B. How many units? What number? More than two.

(v) ALL men are hùman (y + 9), but not all sing. All the men in this room sing. All of them sing. They all sing.

(vi) EVERY word in this book is in the dìctionary. Every word is there. You can find every one. But not every word in the dictionary is in this book.

(vii) Write EACH new word, one by one, in your notebook. Write each one on a sëparate (3) line. Use a separate line for each.

(viii) I go to the library every day. Come to the library one day— ANY day you like. Have you any books on space travel? We haven't any yet.

(ix) We have ONE book now, only one. SOME day we'll have more.

(x) SOME people never answer letters. Are there some letters for me?—I am expècting four or five.

(xi) There is NO answer: NONE. There are no letters for you: none, not one. None of the letters are for you.

C. Which of two?

(xii) Here are two keys. BOTH the keys—both of them, both—are good. Both keys, both my keys, can open my drawer.

(xiii) Here are the two keys. I have one key in EACH hand.

(xiv) EITHER key can open my drawer; either of them.

(xv) But NEITHER key can open my safe: neither of them.

D. How much of a unit?

(xvi) Some people will ünderstand all of this book—the whole book. Others will understand some of it. Others will not understand any of it: they will understand none of it.

(xvii) *Note:* We work all day, sleep all night and breathe all the time.

128. *Fit the following words into the patterns in 127:*

A (i) earth, solid, hard, garden, soft; (ii) food, hungry, bread, fruit, eat; (iii) fruit, sweet, corn, this field, ripe, green; (iv) plants, no soil; B (v) boys, swim, class; (vi) name, list, tèlephone böok; (vii) addrèss, addrèss böok; (viii) and (ix) club, evening, places for new members; (x) send, prèsents; (xi) nèwspaper todäy; C (xii) straps, light, hold my camera, my suitcase; D (xvi) can (can't) transläte, page.

129. *Study; then cover up the right-hand column, look at the left, and repeat the right from memory:*

Instëad of—	we can say:
(*a*) all things; all the things here	èverything; èverything hère
(*b*) all the other things	ëverything èlse

67

(c) all people; all the other people èveryone (or èverybody);
      everyone (etc.) else
(d) any thing; any other thing ànything; änything èlse
(e) any person, any other person ànyone (or anybody); anyone
      (etc.) else
(f) some thing; some other thing sòmething; something else
(g) some person; etc. sòmeone (or somebody); etc.
(h) no thing; etc. nòthing; etc.
(i) the hat of some other person sömebody èlse's hät
(j) These are mine. They belong to These are mine. They are nobody
    no other person else's

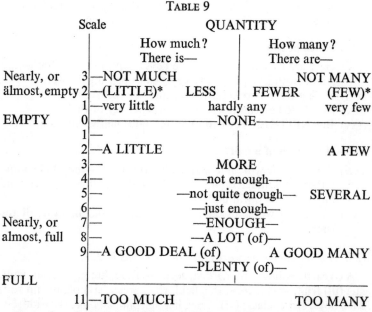

TABLE 9

Scale		QUANTITY	
		How much? There is—	How many? There are—
Nearly, or	3 —NOT MUCH		NOT MANY
älmost, empty	2 —(LITTLE)* LESS		FEWER (FEW)*
	1 —very little	hardly any	very few
EMPTY	0 ——————————NONE——————		
	1 —		
	2 —A LITTLE		A FEW
	3 —	MORE	
	4 —	—not enough—	
	5 —	—not quite enough—	SEVERAL
	6 —	—just enough—	
Nearly, or	7 —	—ENOUGH—	
almost, full	8 —	—A LOT (of)—	
	9 —A GOOD DEAL (of)		A GOOD MANY
		—PLENTY (of)—	
FULL			
	11 —TOO MUCH		TOO MANY

From 3 to 0 there is a dècrease (1) in quäntity. From 0 to 11, an increase. Use the words on the left only for amòunt; the words on the right only for number; the words in the middle for both.

Little and *few* = älmost nòne; *a little* and *a few* = more than none; *too much, too many* = möre than nècessary.

All these words except *none* (see Table 8) can be used with a noun or without. If *a lot, a good deal* and *plenty* are used with a noun, say *a lot of water,* etc. Without a noun, omit *of.*

* *See note.*

130. *Learn Table 9.*

131. *Imagine the line down the left-hand side of Table 9 is a scale marking the amount of a liquid or solid, or the number of objects, in a container. Suppose the container is the petrol tank of a car. The tank holds 10 gallons. We are going on a journey and need about 6 gallons. Read the following:*

(a) When there are only two gallons in the tank, there is not **much.**
(b) When there is only one gallon, there is **very little,** or **hardly any.**
(c) When the tank is empty, there is **none.**
(d) Start filling the tank. There is **a little** in it now.
(e) There is **not enough** yet, **not quite enough.**
(f) Now there is **just enough. Enough. Quite enough.**
(g) There is **a lot.** There is **plenty.**
(h) The tank is full. Stop. Now there is **too much.**

Imagine the container is a packing-case for books (units). Begin: 'When there are only two dozen . . . ' *and continue. Again, imagine it is a sack of rice (mass), and begin:* 'When there are only two pounds . . .'. *Then, imagine it is a box to hold packets of cigarettes, and begin:* 'When there are only two packets . . .'. *Now repeat the whole exercise inserting the noun after the expressions in bold type and making the necessary changes, e.g. there is not much petrol, there are not many books, enough petrol, etc.*

132. *Read. Then cover up the right-hand side, look at the left, and say the right from memory. Then cover up the left, etc., and begin the sentence putting the second part first.*

(a) When there are only 5 gallons in it, | the tank is half empty.
(b) When there is still half a gallon, | it is not quite empty.
(c) When there is only half a gallon, | it is almost empty.
(d) When there is none left, | it is quite empty.
(e) When there are 5 gallons in, | the tank is half full.
(f) When there are 9 gallons in, | it is almost (or nearly) full.
(g) When there only 9 gallons in, | it is not quite full.
(h) When there are 10 gallons in, | it is quite full.
(i) When there are only 4 or 5 gallons in, | it is not nearly full.
(j) When there are 5 gallons, no more, no less, | it is just half full, exactly half full.

(*k*) When there is a little more than
    5, or a little less,   it is about half full.
(*l*) Don't guess. Tell me the ãctual
    amöunt in the tànk.   Five and three-quarter gallons.
(*m*) What is the ãctual fìgure?   5¾ (five and three-quarters).

Table 10

Order of limiting adjectives before a noun

(*a*) a lot of, plenty of, a little, all, any, hardly any, enough, much, not much, more, most, no	white bread hot water good advice	(mass)
any, each, every, no, some	young person—	(unit)
a lot of, plenty of, a few, all, enough, many, more, most, several, some	young people—	(units)

(*b*) all, both, half, twice,		the this	
all, both, half; any, hardly any, a few, few, a little, little; each one, every one; either, neither; enough; much, many, more, most, none; several, some; plenty	of	that these those my your his our their John's	white bread hot water good advice young people

---

133. **We have no hot water. We have plenty of fresh eggs.
      Both the new suits in that cupboard are mine.
      Some of John's English books are missing.**

*Notice how these examples follow the scheme in Table 10. Use Table 10 to make up 20 sensible sentences using **either** a phrase from column 1 (at the beginning of the sentence), **or** a phrase from column 4 (at the end), plus one word or group of words from column 2, and one group of words from column 3:*

70

1	2	3	4
I want	all, both, each,	that brown paper	is broken
You can have	each one of,	those red apples	is torn
There is	every,	hot water	are broken
There are	every one of,	old photographs	are true
	a few, a lot of,	my big suitcases	is useful
	more, most,	John's good advice	are useful
	some, some of,	plate on this table	
	several,	the money in my	
	several of	purse	

How much, how many, how old, how long, etc.

134. *Read, and fill the gaps:*

(*a*) I have a certain amount of money. What amount? Much or little? How much?

(*b*) What is the price of this material? How much does it cost?

(*c*) What is the value of it? How much is it worth?

(*d*) I have a certain — of books. What —? Many or —? How —?

(*e*) What is your age? Are you old or —? How — are you?

(*f*) What is the size of this room? It is big or little? How — — —? Is it large or small? How — — —?

(*g*) What is its length? How — — —? (*h*) its width? How — — —? (*i*) its height? How — — —? (*j*) the weight [13] of this parcel? How — — —? (*k*) the depth of this river? How — — —? (*l*) the strength of this steel? How — — —? (*m*) the thickness of this rope? How — — —? (*n*) the distance from x to y? How far — —? (*o*) the length of this pèriod (18)? How — — —?

135.

Question	*Negative*	*Affirmative*
How much water is there in the tank?	**Not much, not very much.**	**A lot; plenty; a good deal.**
How many eggs are there in the basket?	**Not many, not very many.**	**A lot; plenty; a good many.**
How far is it to the station?	**Not far, not very far.**	**A long way.**
How long is it till Chrìstmas?*	**Not long, not very long.**	**A long time.**

Make up 5 questions on each of these patterns and answer each question, first in the negative, then in the affirmative.

* Chrìstmas (2: ch = k).

136. (a) **I want a piece of wire 8 inches long. This piece is seven and a half inches. It is not long enough: it is too short. That piece is nine inches: it is too long. Ah, this piece is just long enough.**

Repeat with: pole, 8 mètres* high; piece of tape, one inch wide (half an inch, one and a half inches, or an inch and a half); a cushion, ten cëntimetres thick; a piece of meat weighing three kilos (1, 17).

(b) **I want a piece only eight inches long. I don't want a piece as long as that. I don't want it so long. I don't want such a long piece.**

Repeat with the examples given in (a).

137. *Learn Table 11.*

TABLE 11
Degrëe and Compàrison (4)

Tèmperature	Wèather	Temperature	Weather
0 degrèes	very cold	30	very hot
5 ,,	cold	25	hot
10 ,,	not so cold	20	not so hot
	not very cold		not very hot
15 ,,	warmer	15	cooler
20 ,,	warm	10	cool
25 ,,	hot	5	cold
30 ,,	very hot	0	very cold

Notes: 1. *not so cold* = not cold to the same degree (as before), or not cold to an extrëme degrèe.
2. *not very cold* = not cold to an extreme degree.
3. 30 degrees is *the highest* temperature on this scale; 0 is *the lowest.*

---

138. *Look at the scale in Table 11. Then read the sentences below, answer the questions, fill the gaps and follow the instructions in (m):*

(a) Which are the high numbers? Which are the low ones?
(b) 5 is lower than 10; therefore 10 is — — 5.
(c) 25 is a lower number — 30; therefore 30 — — — — — —.
(d) Which is the lower number, 15 or 20? And which is the —?
(e) Which is the lowest number on the scale? And which is the —?
(f) Three times three (3 × 3) is more than twice four (2 × 4).
(g) Three times five is less than four — —.

* mètre: *pronounce as* [mèeter].

72

(*h*) Four twos (4 × 2) are — — three threes (3 × 3).

(*i*) (3 × 4) is as much as (2 × 6): one amount is ëqual (1) to the other.

(*j*) (3 × 5) is not as much as (2 × 9);   (*k*) (4 × 6) is twice as much as (3 × 4);   (*l*) (3 × 6) are half as much as —.

(*m*) Compäre: (4 × 5) and (3 × 7); (6 × 3) and (2 × 9);
(8 × 2) and (3 × 5); (8 × 3) and (5 × 5);
(8 × 4) and (3 × 11).

(*n*) Which is the greater, (6 × 8) or (7 × 7)?

(*o*) Which is the smaller, 6 plus 8, or 23 minus* 9.

(*p*) What is the highest mountain in the world?

(*q*) John (6) has 14 dollars, Pëter (1) has 13, James has 15. Peter has — money than John and also — than James. John has — — Peter, and — — James. John has as — money as Peter, but not — — — James. Who has the most (17)? — — — least?

(*r*) Many people drink coffee, but ëven (1) möre drïnk tèa. In fact, most people drink tea today.

(*s*) We have mäny impörtant thïngs to dò. This is more important than that; therefore that is less important — —. In fact, this is the most important thing of all, and that — — — —.

(*t*) Thank you very much. You are most kind; and you tell a most interesting story. (That is to say, you are kind to the highest degree, and your story is interesting to the highest degree).

139.   *Learn Table 12, and study these notes on it:*

(*a*)   near, nearer, nearest: *use this form of the comparison for words of one syllable.* Near, nearer, nearest *refer to distance.* Next (*123*) *refers to order.*

(*b*)   longer, longest; stronger, strongest; younger, youngest: *Pronounce* ng + g *in all of these words.*

(*c*)   big, bigger; late, later: *see 87, footnote.*

(*d*)   clever, cleverer, cleverest: *use this form of the comparison for words of two syllables when the first is stressed and the second consists of a simple sound such as consonant plus vowel, or l or n, as in* gentle, common.

(*e*)   useful, more useful, most useful: *use this form for all other adjectives of more than one syllable.*

(*f*)   *Note the irregular forms.* Little, less, least *refer to quantity (see Table 9). Do not use the comparative or superlative for* 'little' *meaning* 'small' *but say* smaller, smallest.

(*g*)   *Use* farther, farthest *only for distance:* e.g. The North and South

* mìnus (14).

TABLE 12

Compärison of Àdjectives

Degrèe				
1. Pòsitive (6)	near	long	big	late
2. Compàrative (4)	nearer	longer	bigger	later
3. Supèrlative	nearest	longest	biggest	latest

èarly	clèver	nàrrow	còmmon
èarlier	clèverer	nàrrower	còmmoner
èarliest	clèverest	nàrrowest	còmmonest

ùseful	fòolish	ìnteresting
more useful	more foolish	more interesting
most useful	most foolish	most interesting

Irregular

good	bad, ill	much, many	(a) little	far
better	worse (11)	more	less	⎰ farther ⎱ further
best	worst (11)	most	least	⎰ farthest ⎱ furthest

Poles are the farthest points from the equàtor (13). *Use* further *for distance, or to mean 'one more';* e.g. 'a further question' *means* 'one more question'.

(*h*) *The comparison of* old *is regular, i.e.* older, oldest. *In referring to comparative ages in a family group, use* elder *and* eldest, *but attributively only* (*see* 96). *Examples:*

Attributive	*Predicative*
John is George's elder brother.	John is older than George.
Dr Freeman is the eldest member of the family.	

140. *Give the comparative and superlative of:*

àngry, bad, beaùtiful, cèrtain, cheap, còmmon, dàngerous, deep, èarly, far, fat, fèeble, fèrtile, frèquent (1), good, great, hàppy, hèalthy, ìnteresting, kind, little, long, loud, much, nàrrow, nàtural, nècessary, old, pàinful, poor, pùblic, prìvate (14), quick, quiet, règular, respònsible, sad, safe, sènsible, sèrious (18), shàllow, straight, strong, thin, üncèrtain, ünhèalthy, weak, wet, wise, young. [50]

141. *Read; then cover up the right-hand column, look at the left and repeat the right from memory:*

If something is very cold,	we say it is as cöld as ìce.
,, ,, ,, ,, dry,	,, ,, ,, ,, as dry as dust.
,, ,, ,, ,, hard,	,, ,, ,, ,, as hard as iron.
,, ,, ,, ,, soft,	,, ,, ,, ,, as soft as silk.
,, ,, ,, ,, heavy,	,, ,, ,, ,, as heavy as lead.
,, ,, ,, ,, light,	,, ,, ,, ,, as light as a feather.
,, ,, ,, ,, sharp,	,, ,, ,, ,, as sharp as a knife.
,, ,, ,, ,, old,	,, ,, ,, ,, as old as the hills.
,, a child ,, ,, quiet,	,, ,, ,, ,, as quiet as a mouse.
,, ,, ,, ,, good,	,, ,, ,, ,, as good as gold.

Passages for Reading, Study and Dictation

142.   A letter to a friend

Dëar Jàck,

Mäny thänks for your pòst-card. I'm sörry I can't gö to the màtch with yoú. I have a mönth's hòliday | and am spénding it at my coüsin's färm in the coùntry. Coüsin Röbert (6) is märried (4) and his wífe is a vëry göod hòusewífe. He thïnks her cöoking is the bëst in the wòrld. They are as häppy as sànd böys, | and I'm gläd to be wìth them.

My röom is at the töp of the hòuse, | and it is mùch quïeter hëre than at hòme. This is jüst whät I wànt. I have a löt of rèading to dö, | and there is sö lìttle öpportünity (y + 9) for it düring the tèrm. There are töo mäny òther thïngs to dö. Wòrk nëxt tërm will be fär mòre dìfficult, | and nöw I have tïme to thìnk abòut it.

The pëople hére | gët üp at fíve | and stärt their däy èarly. I dön't gët òut of bëd tïll sèven. Thën I gö for an höur's wàlk, | üsually alöng the rìver-bänk | and häve a swìm—if the wäter is nöt töo cöld. Äfter bréakfast, | I rëad äll the mòrning, | and dön't sëe ànybody. Äfter lúnch, | I explöre the coùntrysïde, | and ëvery ëvening we äll drïve över to the nëxt víllage | to plä gölf with some frïends of Ròbert's. There's nöthing ëlse to dò; | but I enjòy it.

All the best,
John

143.   A bùsiness* lëtter

24, Öxford Ròad,
Frèetown.
16th October, 196–.

Dear Sir,

Thank you for your letter of yesterday's date in answer to mine of October 14th about furniture for my new office. I am now able to send you a firm order.

Please supply:

1. a desk, of the same size, quality and price as the larger one in your shòw-room, and a chair to match;

2. two of your bëst quälity lëather ärm-chàirs;

3. a low round wooden table;

4. two steel cupboards (lockable), each six feet high, three feet wide, and two feet six inches deep, and each with four rows of shelves, of equal height; colour, either black or brown.

I am not ordering any cúrtain matërial (18), as I think I have enoügh for the prèsent (3). But please send me at least twelve different sàmples of matërial, | in cäse I decïde to örder sö me làter.

Yours fáithfully,
T. B. Morris

Messrs. William Harris and Sons,
4, Nórth Street,
Freetown.

TESTS

144. *Put one word in each gap, and make sense of the whole dialogue. Count a word followed by apostrophe s as one.*

(a) — is that noise?   There is — at — door.

(b) — is it?   — the postman.

(c) Good. There — — letters. There — — — tèlegram (3).

(d) — is — important?   — telegram, of course.

(e) Not — telegrams — —.   I agree, but — are; and — one is — —. Read —. Is there — answer?

(f) No, there is — answer.   Now look at — letters. — writing is that?

(g) That is —.   And — is Charles?

* *pronounce* [bìznis].

76

(h) — is a good friend — —. In
fact, he is my — friend. — is
— — — men in — photo-
graph.   — one is he?

(i) — first on the left in — front   And — is the name of the —
row (17).   man?

(j) I don't know — name. Let   All right, I won't (17) ask —
me read — —.   more questions.

(k) Good. Now bring me — to   Tea? Coffee? Or anything —?
drink.

(l) It doesn't matter. Bring me   Here is — lĕmonàde, as cold as
— liquid.   —.

145.   *We can say* 'This cup is clean' *or* 'This is a clean cup'. *We can
say* 'What is your age?' *or* 'How old are you?' *There is very little, or
no, difference in meaning between one expression and the other, although there may be a difference in emphasis. Say the following in a
different but acceptable way, using only the patterns given so far in this
book:*

1. What is that letter?
2. What boy is that?
3. Whose towel is this?
4. That is her towel.
5. The name of your father.
6. The address of your parents.
7. The trunk of an elephant.
8. The side of the road.
9. The work of an evening.
10. I haven't any idea.
11. All the people are happy.
12. Any person can tell you.
13. Ask some other person.
14. There is hardly any time.
15. There are hardly any plates.
16. But there is a lot of bread.
17. There is nothing in the basket.
18. The box is not quite full.
19. This is not the same box.
20. But is it just as big?
21. Answer the question after
this.
22. It is not so warm today.
23. Lead is heavier than tin.

24. (2 × 3) is half as much as
(3 × 4).
25. This is the same length as
that.
26. I am the same age as you.
27. How large is this room?
28. Give me one more.
29. Where are the other people?
30. My two sisters are married.
31. Their husbands are doctors.
32. The life of a doctor is a busy
one.
33. His day is not long enough.
34. This chair is too low.
35. It is higher than the next one.
36. Peter is older than Harold.
37. Harold is Peter's younger
brother.
38. My work is not so good as
yours.
39. Mine is not so bad as his.
40. Yours is the least untidy.
41. I can understand only some of
this.

42. The room is only half full.
43. Here is a further example.
44. This is not public property.
45. This is mine, nobody else's.
46. I don't like tea as weak as this.
47. I don't like such strong coffee.
48. Mr Porter is a teacher of music.
49. Ralph is one of his students.
50. I can't sleep on such a hard bed.

4. STATEMENT, COMMAND AND QUESTION

TABLE 13

Parts of a Sentence

SUBJECT	PREDICATE			
noun (with ádjective) or prònoun	*verb*	*còmplement*	*òbject*	*àdverb*
Bïrds	flỳ.			
My yoünger bröther	is	an àrchitect.		
He	dräws		plàns.	
The pëople in this coüntry	wörk			hàrd.
It	is	làte.		
Yoü	sït			dòwn!
(You)	Stànd!			

146. *Study Table 13, and make up other sentences on the same patterns. Give every sentence a* **subject** *and a* **verb**. *The verb must be* **finite** *(14, 14), i.e. either in the* **indicative** *(2) form or the* **impèrative** *(3): see Tables 14–17.*

TABLE 14

The verb TO BE

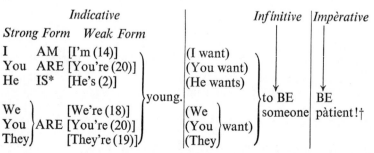

	Indicative		*Infinitive*	*Impèrative*
Strong Form	*Weak Form*			
I AM	[I'm (14)]			
You ARE	[You're (20)]	(I want)		
He IS*	[He's (2)]	(You want)		
		(He wants)		
		young.	to BE	BE
We	[We're (18)]	(We	someone	pàtient!†
You ARE	[You're (20)]	(You want)		
They	[They're (19)]	(They		

* In all verbs, he, she *and* it *take the same form.*
† pàtient (13: ti = sh).

79

TABLE 15

The verb TO HAVE

Indicative				Infinitive	Imperative
I		[I've (14)]		(I	
You	HAVE	[You've]		(You	want)
We		[We've]	a	(We	to HAVE
They		[They've]	name.	(They	a drink. HAVE it!
He	HAS	[He's]*		(He wants)	

Say He's got, to avoid confusion with the weak form of He is.

147. *Learn Tables 14 and 15 by heart.*

TABLE 16

Mòdal (17) Vërbs

I, you, he, we, they { CAN / MUST } be patient!

(No infinitive. No imperative.)

148. *Learn Table 16 by heart.*

TABLE 17

Full verbs

Indicative		Infinitive	Imperative
I, you, we, they SEE	(We want)	TO SEE	SEE for yourself!
He SEES	(He wants)		

149. *Learn Table 17 by heart. USE IT FOR 'FULL' VERBS, i.e.*
ALL VERBS in English excëpt be *and* have, *and* can, must, will *and*
the few other auxïliary and modal verbs in Chäpter 7. Now study Table
18.

TABLE 18

Plural of Nouns			Verbs	
			Infinitive	3rd Person Singular
				Sound of ending
Soft sounds		trees, pens	play, run	He plays, runs [z]
Hard		hats, books	stop, put, take	He stops, puts, takes [s]
Hissing sounds	(piece)	pieces	dance	He dances [iz]
	(match)	matches	touch (10)	He touches [iz]
	(box)	boxes	wash	He washes [iz]
Consonant/y	(city)	cities	try	He tries [z]
Ending in o	(hero)	heroes	go	He goes [z]
			do (9)	He does (10) ⎫ excep-
			say (13)	He says (3) ⎭ tions

150. *Say and spell the 3rd Person Singular (e.g.* he plays) *of the following verbs:* eat, drink, win, lose (9 + z), go, stay, laugh (5 + f), cry, hit, miss, join, mix, bring, fetch, dress, brush, enjòy, amùse, còpy, bùry (3). [20]

151. *Learn the following verbs and give the 1st, 2nd and 3rd person singular of each one:*

(a) *Mövements* (9) *of the bòdy:*

start	put (8)	bend	throw (17)
stop	take	stretch	catch
go	push (8)	turn	hold
come	pull (8)	twist	drop
hùrry (10)	press	touch (10)	keep (something)
wait	draw	rub	let (something) go
run	give (2)	shake	climb (14: *b silent*)
walk	get	break (3)	slip
jump	send	tear (19)	stand
fall	recèive (1)	bite	sit [40]

(b) *Acts of the senses:*

look, listen (*i.e. give your attèntion with eyes, or ears*);
see, hear (*i.e. recèive an imprèssion on the sènses*);
feel, smell, taste (*i.e. either give attention or receive an impression*);
like, love (10), want. [10]

(c) *Mental acts:*

know	believe (1)*	remember	mean	hope	agree
think	doubt	forget	understand	wish	prefer
		wonder (10)	[15]		

152. *Fill each gap with a verb from 151. Use as many of the verbs as you can:*

(a) Let's — at the beginning. In the morning, I wake up, — my eyes, — out of bed, — my feet on the cold floor, and — to the window. I — there, — the fresh air on my face, and — my arms.

(b) —. Can you — that music? —. Can you — the new moon? — this coffee: is there soap in it? Can you — gas?

(c) A. This ice is dangerous. You can ëasily — on it. B. I — ; you're right. — at my wrist. It's very painful. Don't — it. I — I have broken a bone.

(d) Here is a letter. — it, — to the post-office, — a stamp, stick the stamp on the envelope, and — the letter in the box. —. Here is some money for the stamp. Don't — it. — it in your pocket.

(e) — with me to the post-office. I must — a telegram. Don't —. There's plenty of time. There's no need to —.

(f) A. Who is that, I —. Is it Árthur? B. I — it is, but I'm not sure. A. I — it's Paul (7). Yes, now I'm certain, I — it's Paul.

(g) I can't — this word. What does it —?

(h) What can we do with paper? We can — it. With glass? We can — it. With a piece of rubber? We can — it, — it, and — it. What can we do with chòcolate? We can — it. We — clothes, and — water from a well.

(i) A. — me the key of the cupboard. Don't — it: I can't —. Thank you. But I can't open the door. B. You must — the key twice, then — the door, and —.

(j) How high can you —? Can you — a mountain?

(k) I — something to drink. I don't — coffee. I — tea.

(l) — that man! Don't — him go. — him to prison.

(m) That's enough. I — that's all. I — you a Häppy Nëw Yèar. [60]

153. *Study.*

(a) *Some words are both nouns which refër to an actïvity in géneral, and verbs which tell us what the subject dòes; e.g.*

Wörk is a üseful actïvity. Most men work.

Play is a pleasure. Children play.

Slëep is nècessary. We sleep at night.

* *Note the spelling of* believe *and* receive. *The rule of thumb, 'i before e except after c,' applies to a number of words of similar type, e.g.* relieve, deceive.

(*b*) *Some words are both verbs, and nouns which refer to a single act; e.g.*

I walk home in the evening, and go for a walk on Sundays.
Some people have a little sleep after lunch.

(*c*) *Many words are nouns which refer to things, and also verbs; e.g.*

Where there is smoke, there is fire. You smoke too much!
A vegetable is a plant. We plant vegetables in soft soil.
Please lock the door. I can't, there is no lock on it.
One* drinks a lot in hot weather. Have a drink now!

(*d*) *Some words can be both adjectives and verbs; e.g.*

The door is ópen (17), the window is shut.
Shut the door, open the window.
Clean this floor and dry it.
It is neither clean nor dry.

154. *Study. We can always form a kind of noun from verbs by adding* -ing *to the infinitive. The form ending in* -ing *can be called the verbal noun or gerund: it refers to action or pròcess. Examples:*

Wälking and swïmming are böth göod èxercise.
Too much smoking is bad for your lungs.
Young people like singing† and dancing.†

155. *Learn the examples in paragraphs 153 and 154. Say which words in those examples are used as* (*a*) *nouns,* (*b*) *adjectives,* (*c*) *verbs, and* (*d*) *verbal nouns.*

156. *Study. Sometimes a noun ends in a hard consonant which is soft in the corresponding verb: e.g.*

Nouns	Verbs
life (14), breath (3), use,	live (2), breathe (1), use,
excùse, house, advìce,	excùse, house, advìse,
proof (9), belièf	prove (9), belière

In práctice (4 + 2: *noun*) *and* pràctise (4 + 2: *verb*) *the final consonant is pronounced the same* (*hard*). *Corresponding to the noun* bath (*hard*) *there are two verbs:* bath (*hard*) *and* bathe (13, *soft*). *From the verb* bathe *we can then form a noun,* bathe (*soft*), *e.g. We bathe in the sea* (*or have a bathe*) *and bathe a wound, but bath a baby. Note the*

* *We can say* People drink . . . *or* we drink . . . *or* you drink . . . *or* one drinks . . .

† *Note the spelling of:* swim, swimming; dance, dancing. *This is in accordance with the rule given in the footnote to* 87. *Do not pronounce any separate g sound after the ng sounds in* singing: *compare* 139 (b).

adjective close (*hard s*) *and the verb* close (*soft s*): My house is close (*adj.*) to the sea. I must close (*verb*) the windows when the sea is rough. *Sometimes a noun is accented on the first of two syllables, and the corresponding verb is accented on the second:*

Nouns	Verbs
rècord, ìmport, èxport	recòrd, impòrt, expòrt

157. *Fill each gap by a noun or verb from 156:*

 (*a*) We — in an interesting world. — is interesting.

 (*b*) Always — through your nose. Take a deep —.

 (*c*) A. I'm sorry, — me. B. I accëpt your —.

 (*d*) A. I need your —. B. Then I — you to stop smoking.

 (*e*) — your verbs. Do half an hour's — every day.

 (*f*) I understand the — of the articles, but I can't — many verbs yet.

 (*g*) I — you are right. That is my —. But I have no —. I can't — it.

 (*h*) We — people in houses. Which is your —?

 (*i*) We have a — in the bathroom. We — in the sea, — a wound, and — the baby.

 (*j*) It's cold in here. — the door and sit — to the fire.

 (*k*) When we — a speech, we put it on —.

 (*l*) Traders — certain foods. Those are called —. They — other goods. Those are called —. [30]

158. **A swïmmer is a përson who swïms.**
Workers are people who work.
A cär-driver is a përson who drïves a càr.
Höuse owners are pëople who öwn hòuses.

Use one of these patterns with each of the words below:

advìser	mèat ëater	shòpkeepers	readers
begìnners*	farmers	killer	recèiver
believer	fighters	lèaders (1)	hòrse rïders
buïlders	finder	learners	ruler
buyers	flier	lìsteners	runners*
callers	fòllower	loser	bòokseller
mòney-chänger	giver	mùsic lover	singers
cleaners	frùit gröwers	shòemakers	smokers
climber	helper	hòuse owner	pìpe smöker
dancers	fòod impörters	teà-plänter	speaker
bùs-drïvers	intèrpreter	tènnis pläyer*	teachers
wàge-ëarner	bèe keeper	piàno pläyer*	thinker

tràveller*	winners*	actor	protèctors
walkers	worker	beggars	sailors
watcher	writers	stàmp-collëctor	vìsitor [60]

159. *Do Exercise 158 again, putting the singular words into the plural, and vice versa* (14; 11, 12).

160. *In a few cases the same word is used for the verb and the noun referring to the person who performs the action;* e.g. cook, guard, guide, judge: a cook cooks, etc. *On the other hand,* a cooker is an apparatus or pot for cooking, a roller is something which rolls a soft substance flat. *Note:* a swimmer is someone who . . . , a roller is something which . . .

161. *Answer:* What is a cook, a guard, a guide, a judge, a heater, a leader, a tìn-öpener, a tàpe-recörder, a cigarètte lìghter, a scrèwdrïver, a tràin drïver, a wïse rùler, a wöoden rùler, a spàce tràveller, a bìrd wätcher?

Agreement of Subject and Verb

162. **One of the light bulbs is broken.**
Öxygen (6, 2, 12) and hÿdrogen (14) are gàses (4).
Oxygen, like hydrogen, is a gas.
Our family has its own house.
Our family have their own house.

Put the verb into the singular or plural:

(a) (be) The news (*see 68 g*) — very good today.
(b) (be) Some people — thoughtful, others — thoughtless.
(c) (have) The commïttee — their meeting every Friday.
(d) (be) The full story of these evënts — on rècord.
(e) (want) The gövernment (10) — its own way.
(f) (be, make) 16 and 18 — 34. Blue and yellow — green.
(g) (have) One of those men — a gun.
(h) (have) Each family — — own house.
(i) (have) Everybody — — own likes and dìslikes.
(j) (be) All the milk in these bottles — sour.

* *Note the spelling of* begìn, begìnner; run, runner; win, winner: (*see footnote to* 87). *Note* tràvel, tràveller, tràvelling, *although the second syllable in* travel *is not the stressed one. Note also that* we play tennis (a game) *but* play the piano (a musical instrument).

85

Complëting the Prèdicate

163. (a) *The verb* to be (*also* become *and* seem) *must have a còmplement:*

Sùbject	Verb	Còmplement
My bröther	is	an àrchitect.
		vëry bùsy (2).
		in the nëxt ròom.
He	sëems (or löoks)	tìred.

(b) *Some verbs must have an* **òbject;** *e.g.*

		Object
My üncle	häs	a càr.
He	owns (17)	a hòuse.
Yoü	can transläte	thïs sèntence.

(c) *In some contexts, a verb needs an* **àdverb,** *or adverb phrase* (*answering the question* how, where *or* when) *to complete the sense, e.g.*

	Adverb
You wrïte	clèarly.
Geörge wörks	in an òffice.
He wörks	äll dày.

(d) *Verbs need a subject, and this is sometimes supplied by* **it;** *e.g.* It is early, it's late (light, dark, cold, hot, raining, snowing). It doesn't matter. It seems to me . . .

(e) *Note the example in 60:* There is a pencil in your pocket; *and, on the same pattern,* There is plenty to eat. There are many people in the world.

The Direct Object

164. *See 163* (b). *Verbs which take an object are called* **trànsitive.** *Those that do not, like* come *or* go, *are* **ìntrànsitive.** *Some verbs can be transitive or* **intransitive,** *accòrding to the sense; e.g.*

Birds fly (*intransitive*). Men fly àeroplanes (*transitive*). *Note that* lie (14) *and* rise *are intransitive only:* lay *and* raise *are only transitive. Examples:*

Don't lie on the wet ground.
The sun and the moon rise at different times.
Lay the ïnjured (2, 12) man gently on the ground. Raise his head a little.

165. *The personal pronouns* (Table 7) *change in form when they are the object of the verb. They are then said to be in the* **objëctive càse.** *When a personal pronoun is the subject of the sentence, it is said to be in the* **nòminative** (6) *case. The personal pronouns, and* who,* *are the only words in English which change their form in this way. See and learn Table 19.*

TABLE 19
Personal Pronouns: Case

Nòminative		*Objèctive*	
WHO (9)	sees	WHOM (9)?	
I	see	YOU	(*2nd person*)
You	see	ME	(*1st, singular*)
We	see	HIM	(*3rd, singular, masculine*)
He	sees	HER	(*3rd, singular, feminine*)
They	see	US	(*1st, plural*)
We	see	THEM	(*3rd, plural*)

(It *is the same in both cases*)

Always use the objective case after prepositions, e.g. to, from, on, in, by, with, of, between, etc. *Examples:* Give that to me. Between you and me.

Reflëxive Prònouns

166. *When the subject and the object of a verb are the same person, we use the* **reflëxive prònouns,** myself, yourself, himself, *etc. for the object. Examples:*

I löse MYSELF in a stränge cìty. (*Stress:* I lòse myself)
Enjòy YOURSELF. Behàve (13) YOURSELF! (singular)
Nöbody can sëe HIMSELF as òthers see him.
A wöman löoks at HERSELF in a mìrror.
A cät wáshes ITSELF, and amùses itself.
We drÿ OURSELVES with a tòwel.
Dön't decèive (1) YOURSELVES. (plural)
Söme people kïll THEMSELVES with wòrry (10).
Note: Twö pëople mèet EACH OTHER. Möre than two people mèet ONE ANOTHER.

* Who *often remains unchanged even when it is the object. Use* whom (*a*) *when you wish to emphasise that you are referring to the object* (e.g. Who beat whom?) *or* (*b*) *after a preposition.*

167. *Use* myself, yourself, *etc. also to give emphasis to the subject, e.g.*

Whö drïves this càr? Ì drïve it. I drïve it mysèlf.
Yoü are a páinter? Höw ìnteresting! Ì am a päinter mysèlf. I päint mysèlf. *i.e.* Ì päint tòo.
He cüts his häir himsèlf. *i.e.* He cuts his own hair.
I thïnk you are wròng mysélf | — thät is mỳ opïnion. Yoü yoursèlf are quïte süre you are rìght.

Direct and Indirect Object

168. *In 163 (b)* a car, a house, this sentence *are* **direct objects.**

(*a*) *The verb* ask *can have two direct objects, e.g.*

$$
\text{I ask} \begin{cases} \text{a question. 'What is the price?' I ask the price.} \\ \text{somebody. I ask the shopkeeper.} \\ \text{somebody a question. I ask the shopkeeper the price.} \end{cases}
$$

But note: I want a loaf. I ask the baker for a loaf.

(*b*) Call, make, appoint *can have a direct object followed by a noun in apposition to it, e.g.*

> We call this material plastic.
> We make the right man President.
> We appoint him President for four years.

(*c*) *Other verbs take a direct object and an* **indirect object.** *Learn the following patterns:*

Pattern 1.

	Give WHAT		To WHOM?
a.	„	this lëtter	to the mànager (4).
b.	„	it	to the manager.
c.	„	that letter	to me.
d.	„	it	to me.

Pattern 2.	*Indirect Object*	*Direct Object*
	Give WHOM	WHAT?
a.	„ the mänager	this lètter.
b.	(Do not use the equivalent to Pattern 1 b.)	
c.	„ me	that letter.
d.	„ me	it.

169. *If you have to choose between Pattern 1 and Pattern 2 in 168:*

(*a*) *put the emphasis at the end; e.g.*

Gïve this lëtter to the mànager (to nöbody èlse).
Gïve the mänager this lètter (nöt thät bòok).

(*b*) *put the longer phrase after the shorter one; e.g.*

Gïve   thïs létter | to the Mänager of the Nätional (4) Bànk.
Gïve   the Mánager | thëse thrëe ürgent lètters.

170. (a) **Where is your book? Shòw me.**
      What is your name? Tell me.

The indirect object can stand alone, without a direct object, after show *and* tell.

(b) **Spëak Ènglish (Tälk sènse, Expläin this sèntence) to me.**
     Expläin to us höw this machïne wòrks. Explàin it.

Use speak, talk *and* explain *with Pattern 1 in 168, but not with Pattern 2, nor with the pattern in 170 (a).*

171. *Learn the examples in 163–170, and make up other examples on the same patterns.*

172. *Fill each gap with a suitable pronoun so as to make sense:*

(*a*) This box is too heavy. I can't lift —. Please help —.
(*b*) I can't lift it —. Perhaps — and — can lift — together.
(*c*) It's no use. There are too many books in —. Take some of —
out.
(*d*) Let — help — now. — can do — together. Let — both try.
(*e*) Whose books are — ? Yours and mine. — belong to —.
(*f*) Stop that man! Hold —! Don't let — go!
(*g*) We know —. — is a thief. — gives — a lot of trouble.
(*h*) One of our tyres is flat. — can mend —? We can mend — —.
(*i*) Be careful! — is very muddy. Don't make — dirty.
(*j*) I like her, and — likes me. In fact, — like — — very much.
(*k*) We trust them, and — trust —. — trust — — completely.
(*l*) We want to hear the news. Read — to —. Tell —. Explain —.
(*m*) I need those papers. Find — and bring — to — at once.
(*n*) Your friend is not well. — must take care of —.
(*o*) Some people take too much care of —. — are selfish.
(*p*) The police are outside. — want to come in. Let — come.
(*q*) Listen to the news. — is important. The people are worried. —
want to know the truth. [50]

173. Bring, fetch, give, hand, lend, òffer, owe (17), pass, pay, pròmise (6, 2), read, sell, send, show, take, teach, tell, throw, wish, write.

Use these verbs and the patterns in paragraph 168 to make up 20 sentences with the words or phrases given below. Use a different verb every time, and supply to *if necessary:*

(a) a cup of coffee, me

(b) the truth, them

(c) it, him

(d) a rope, the man on the quay*

(e) your tïcket, the tïcket-collector

(f) some flowers, your wife

(g) that newspaper article, us

(h) my clothes, the dry-clèaners

(i) your mother, the bread

(j) some money for a hàir-cut, him

(k) a letter of thanks, your host (17)

(l) that piece of string, me

(m) the money, the cashíer (18), not to me

(n) a Häppy Nëw Yèar, you all

(o) English, your students

(p) a shílling, you

(q) your paper, the exàminer at the back of the hall

(r) something to drink, your visitors

(s) you, an apòlogy (6)

(t) the way to the garage, Mr Bàiley (13, 2) [20]

174. Say *means* 'speak a word or words', *or* 'make a statement'. Tell *means* 'give information, or an account of something, to somebody'. Tell *fits into Patterns 1 and 2 in paragraph 168,* say *only into Pattern 1. Fill each gap with* say *or* tell:

(a) — 'She sells sea-shells.'

(f) Can you — me the time?

(b) — us the latest news.

(g) Don't — that story to me.

(c) — the inspëctor the truth.

(h) Be quiet. Don't — that.

(d) Please — that again.

(i) Why? Because I — so.

(e) — good-night to your parents.

(j) Do what I — you.

175. **Gët a tïcket for mè. Gët me a tïcket.**

Use the **two** *patterns in 168 (but using* for *instead of* to) *with:*

(a) Get, a chair, Mr Rose; (b) Fetch, that new book, me; (c) I'll buy, it, you; (d) Order, a copy, yourself; (e) Can you build, a house, us? (f) No, but I can make, a cake, you; (g) Will you find, a seat, Mary? (h) Yes, and I'll pick some roses, her. (i) I'll choose a few red ones, myself. (j) Save some, me. [10]

* *Pronounce* [kee].

Adverbs

176. **a. Wïpe the wïndscreen clèan. Këep it clèan.**
      b. You must sëe the röad clèarly.
      c. Be careful. Drive slowly and change gear carefully.

Clean, *in a.*, *is an adjective* (*see 86*) *saying what condition the windscreen must be in.* Careful, *in c.*, *is also an adjective, saying what your behaviour must be like.* Clearly, slowly *and* carefully *are **adverbs**, saying how you must* see, drive, *etc. An **adverb of manner** tells how the subject acts. As a general rule, form adverbs of manner by adding* -ly *to an adjective. Note the spelling when the adjective ends—*

  in -l: èqual (1), èqually; careful, carefully;
  in -le, *preceded by a consonant:* able, ably; gentle, gently;
  in -y: happy, happily; gay, gaily; day, daily.
  in -ic: scïentìfic, scïentìfically; äutomàtic,* äutomàtically;
  in -e: *follow the rule, except with* true, truly; whole, wholly (17).

Exception: adjective, good; *adverb,* well.

177. **That is a lìkely evënt—it will pröbably (6) hàppen.**
     A friendly man acts in a friendly way (or friëndly mànner).

When an adjective already ends in -ly, *e.g.* fatherly, friendly, likely, *use an adverb formed from a word of similar meaning, or use an adverbial phrase. However,* early *can be used as an adverb as well as an adjective:* An early riser rises early.

178.   **A läte stärter is a përson who stärts làte.**
         This is härd wòrk. We must trÿ hàrd.
         A fäst rünner rüns fàst. Aïm hìgh. Lìe lòw.

Late, hard, fast, high, low, far, near *are used both as adjectives and as adverbs. However,* we can speak highly of someone, i.e. praise him; *and* a story can be highly amusing, i.e. amusing to a high degree. Lowly *is an adjective referring to a low position in society.* Hardly *and* nearly *are adverbs of degree* (*see Table 9*); *and* lately *means* 'in rëcent (1) times'.

179. *Adverbs are, as a rule, 'compared' like the longer adjectives in Table 12.*

  Positive: I write carelessly.
  Comparative: You write more quickly.
  Superlative: John writes the most neatly.

* *Pronounce* 7, 12, 4, 2.

Exceptionally, the adverbs late, hard, fast, high, low, near, *also* early *and* soon, *are compared like the shorter adjectives in Table 12.*

I get up early, and work hard.
You get up earlier, and work harder.
John gets up the earliest, and works the hardest.

Special cases: well, better, best; badly, worse, worst; far (*as in Table 12*).

180.   **A fäir jüdge jüdges fàirly.**
        A cäreful cär driver drïves a cär càrefully.

Use one of these patterns with: a more careful driver; a dangerous driver; a hard worker; a cheerful giver; a fast runner; a faster runner; a simple writer; a good writer; a bad writer; a worse writer; the wisest judge; a friendly adviser; an able ruler; true lovers; a harmless weed killer; a clear speaker; the clearest speakers; a patient listener; a scientific explorer; a good football-player; a faithful follower; slow starters; heavy cigarette smokers; a natural actor; late comers; early risers; earlier risers; the gentlest players; the highest bidder; an honest money-changer. [30]

181.   (*a*) *An **adverb of place** tells us where the activity takes place;* e.g. We have our meals *here*. We have them *in the garden*.

(*b*) *An **adverb of time** tells us when;* e.g. Summer begins *today*.

(*c*) *An **adverb of quantity** or **extént** (cf. Table 9) tells us to what extent the activity is performed;* e.g.

He eats *enough*, drinks *very little* and sleeps *too much*.
Stop *a little*. I can't do *more*. I can't go any *farther*.

Note that little, a little, much *and* far *are compared as in Table 12.*

(*d*) *An **adverb of degree** tells us how far an act is completed;* e.g.

He *hardly* says a word. In fact, he can *hardly* speak.
I *quite* understand. I *fully* agree.
I can *just* hear you. I can *nearly* reach the ceiling.

(*e*) *An **adverb of fréquency** or **relative time** tells us how often or at what distance of time an act is performed;* e.g. àlways, gènerally, ùsually, òften, sòmetimes, sèldom, ràrely, nèver; soon, rècently (1).
Note: soon, sooner, soonest; oftener *or* more often.

(*f*) Still, yet, already; *examples:*

At 10 o'clock. Your coat is wet: so is mine.
At 10.15. Yours is already dry. Mine is still wet: it is not yet dry.

182. *An adverb can also modify a numeral, an adjective or another adverb, e.g.*

It is *about* six o'clock. You are *very* kind, *too* good, *äbsolütely* rìght. You do that *very* well, *really most* carefully. In fact, you're *räther* wònderful, but you're not quick *enough*.

183. *Fill each gap with a suitable adverb, so as to make sense of each group of sentences:*

(*a*) Your writing is not good —. You must do —.

(*b*) You are — fat. You eat — —. Eat —.

(*c*) John is — good. He — does his work —, though he is — — slow. He must work —.

(*d*) George — brushes his teeth properly, and he — forgets to brush them at all.

(*e*) The tank is — empty. There is — any water in it.

(*f*) Now it is — empty. It is — dry.

(*g*) In northern Europe, it gets dark — in summer. It is — light at nine o'clock. But it gets dark — in winter: it is — dark at five. It is three o'clock now. It is not dark —.

(*h*) Bring the paper a little —. I can — read it. [25]

Position of Adverbs

184. (a) **You spëak Ënglish vëry wèll.**
  Yöur pläce is thère. Thère is your pläce.
  We have a hòliday todäy. Todáy we have a hòliday.

DO NOT PUT ANYTHING BETWEEN THE VERB AND ITS OBJECT. Put all adverbs, except those of degree and frequency, after the verb and after the object. However, adverbs can also be placed at the beginning of the sentence, especially to give emphasis or to provide a setting in place or time for the statement that follows.

  (b) **It öften ràins here, but it's nëver vëry còld.**
  You must älways täke a ràin-cöat with you.

Put adverbs of degree and frequency before the verb if it consists of a single word, but after the verb to be, *and between a modal verb and its infinitive. See also examples in 181 (d) and 181 (f). Often* can come at *the end of a sentence, for the sake of emphasis; and* sometimes can *come at the beginning of the sentence as well as at the end.* Yet *often comes at the end. Examples:* It rains here often. Sometimes you must wear rubber boots. It is not dry yet.

93

(c) **We häve our mëals hère nöw.**
We üsually ëat in the gärden in sùmmer-time.

If an adverb of place and an adverb of time occur in a sentence together, put the adverb of place first.

(d) **You are quïte rìght. I drïve töo quìckly.**

When an adverb modifies an adjective or another adverb, put it before the word it modifies. However, put enough *after an adjective or adverb; e.g.* That is nöt gòod enoügh. You dön't wrïte clèarly enoügh.

185. *In the following sentences, put a suitable adverb of degree or relative time in the normal position:*

(*a*) Aeroplanes land here.   (*b*) They arrive at midnight.
(*c*) They arrive on time.   (*d*) They fall in the sea.
(*e*) We can see Mars.   (*f*) We have a fog in winter.
(*g*) It is time to go home.   (*h*) I agree with you.
(*i*) We must be serious.   (*j*) You take life seriously. [10]

The General Aspect and the Continuous Aspect of the Verb

The Ordinary Present Tense (as in Table 17, first column).

We write with a pen or pencil.

186. *Fill each gap with a suitable verb:*

(*a*) We — on our own feet.   (*b*) We — with our teeth.
(*c*) We — with our tongue.   (*d*) We — air into our lungs.
(*e*) We — on chairs.   (*f*) We — up ladders.
(*g*) We — things with knives.   (*h*) We — photographs with a camera.

(*i*) The sun — in the east.   (*j*) It — in the west. [10]

187. *Repeat the following as a dialogue. Speaker A gives a command, Speaker B obeys, completes the action and speaks at the same time. Then A repeats the command, B obeys it again but without speaking, and C comments on B's action.**

A. Shüt your bòok!   B. I shüt my bòok.   C. He shuts his book.

Continue with: Put it down. Stand up. Open the door. Now shut it. Switch on the light. Switch it off. Sit down. Pick up your book. Open it. Put it on the table. [10]

* See note.

188.   **We üsually gö öut on Sùnday.**

Fill each gap with a suitable word or phrase:

We always — on Monday. We generally — on Tuesday. We occasionally — on Wednesday. We often — on Thursday. We sometimes — on Friday. We never — on Saturday afternoon.

189.   *Use the Ordinary Present Tense of the verb to express the idea of*

(a) *the activity in general (186);*

(b) *an act completed at the time of speaking (187);*

(c) *a whole series of acts repeated regularly, occasionally, often, always, etc., in present time (188).*

Note: this Tense is a 'simple' one, i.e. it is composed of one word only.

The Present Continuous Tense

190.   *Repeat the following as a dialogue. A gives a command, B obeys it and speaks WHILE THE ACTION IS IN PROGRESS, i.e. after the action starts and before it finishes. Then A repeats the command, B obeys it again and C comments while the action is in progress.*

A. Löok öut of the window. B. I AM LÖOKING öut of the window.

C. HE IS LOOKING out of the window.

Continue with: Walk round the room. Touch your chin. Rub your eyes. Do that again. Speak English. Watch my hand. Move your head. Think of a number. Hold this watch to your left ear. Listen to it. Write your name and address. Look at page 24. Read it. Draw a map of Africa. Put in the chief rivers. [15]

191.   *The Present Continuous Tense is a compound one composed of the Present Tense of* be *(called the* **auxiliary***) plus the form of the verb ending in* -ing. *The* -ing *form is called the* **present pàrticiple** *when it is used in this way. In form it is the same as the gerund (154) and it remains unchanged. See the footnotes to 154 and 158, and spell the present participle of:* run, rub, move, write, rain, hold, put, begín, refér, occúr, prefér, súffer, trável, beliéve, intèrpret.

Note: try, trying; applý, applỳing; die, dying; lie, lying.

192.   **We are bùsy. WE ARE HÄVING a lèsson.**

Use this pattern in the 1st Person Plural with: learn, English; study, for an exäminàtion; do, our best; make, good prògress; get better;

95

impröve (9), all the time; grow, older. *Begin with different introduction instead of* 'We are busy'; e.g. Don't worry (10), *or* We're tired. *Repeat with* you are —, he is —, she is —, they are —.

193. (a) **I üsually gët üp at sèven, | but I AM GETTING UP at six thïs wëek, | to revïse for my exäminàtion.**

Repeat with: we, George, Mary, George and Mary.

(b) **The people next door ARE ALWAYS QUARRELLING.***

Repeat with: that child, playing the piano; old man, asking for money; you, looking at the clock; vïsitors, börrowing my bòoks; I, trying to gët them bàck.

194. *Use the Present Continuous Tense to emphasise the idea of:*

    (*a*) *activity in progress (190, 192).*
    (*b*) *a temporary habit (193 a).*
    (*c*) *a constant, unending habit (193 b).*

Note the idea of incompletion expressed by this tense: in (a), the activitity is still in progress, not complete; in (b), we are not concerned with a regular habit, but with a temporary one—a partial series of acts; in (c), the habit is unending and therefore incomplete.

195. *We can imagine activity in progress more easily with some forms of activity than with others. We can easily imagine it with* look, listen, work, study, play, walk; *less easily with* switch on a light, shut a book, see, hear, know, remember. *You can apply Exercise 190 to* look *and* listen; *but do not apply it to the verbs in 151 (b) when they refer to receiving an impression on the senses, nor to* like, love, want, *nor the verbs in 151 (c). Use these words only in the Simple Present Tense until you can appreciate the subtleties of meaning which are expressed when they are used in the Present Continuous. Note the difference between:* You are having a lesson (*emphasis on activity in progress*) and You have brown eyes (*no such emphasis*).

Interrogative and Negative

196. *Learn Table 20. Form 20 questions on each of these patterns, using different words from those in brackets.*

(*a*) *Then form questions to get the following answers:*

Yes, I'm ready. Yes, I can see it. Geòrge is äbsent. At home. No, he's nöt ïll. No, we're not late. The Smìths are. Yes, we must stop

* *quárrel* (6), *quàrrelling; cf. travel, travelling* (158 b).

TABLE 20

Questions

Auxiliary and Modal Verbs

Statements	Questions to identify the subject	All other Questions Put the verb before the subject.	
I am (sorry).	Whò is (sörry)? (Ì am.)	ÄM I (láte)?	WHY AM Ì (so tired)?
I am (study)ing.	Whò is (study)ing? (Ì am.)	ÄM I (mäking prógress)?	WHÄT AM I (dò)ing?
We are (go)ing.	Whò are (gò)ing? (We are.)	ÀRE WE (móv)ing?	Whère ÀRE WE (gò)ing?
(Dinner) is (ready).	Whàt is (rëady)? (Dinner is.)	IS (DÌNNER rëady)?	Whèn IS (DÌNNER rëady)?
You can (say that).	Whò can (sãy that)? (Yoù can.)	CÄN YOU (sãy thàt)?	Höw CAN YOU (sãy thàt)?
He must (buy it).	Whò must (büy it)? (Hè must.)	MÜST HE (büy it)?	Whàt MUST HE (büy)?

now. No, you can't go yet. John can. Yes, it's most useful. The clòck is bröken. Yes, it's warm inside. Because it's snowing. He must wrïte a repòrt. My name is —. I am very well, thank you. I am twenty-two. The time is half-past six. The date is August 8th. [20]

(b)   **What are you doing? I'm studying.**

Form questions to get the following answers:

He's washing. They're playing tennis. Yes, we're moving fast. She's eating a peach. No, we're working. They're going to a football match. I'm making a radio set. No, I'm making a radio set. Because I want to do it. Because it is a useful language. Because I've no chair. Because this story is so funny. [12]

197.   **A. Thëre is your bàg. Ïs your bäg thére? Whÿ is your bäg thère? B. There is plënty to dò. Ïs there müch to dó? Whÿ is there plënty to dò?**

Use the two question-patterns in (A) or the two in (B), with each of the following:

(*a*) Thëre is my wàtch. (*b*) There is some brëad on the tàble. (*c*) Here is the doctor. (*d*) Here are the police. (*e*) There is a policeman at the door. (*f*) There are some soldiers at the gate. (*g*) There are the soldiers. (*h*) There are a lot of people in the street. (*i*) There are several good plays to see. (*j*) There are the tickets. [10]

198.   *Learn Table 21. Using the patterns in Table 21, form questions to get the following answers:*

Yes, I know the Joneses. Yes, I like them very much. They live next door to me. They both drive their car. Carefully. He wàlks to his öffice. They stay at home, or sometimes go to the theatre. Because they like it. They see actors. The play lasts about two hours. I speak Italian but not Spanish. Yes, I wear glasses for reading. No, I never smoke. Yes, he smokes cigars. He smokes a cigar after dinner. They want clothes. H-U-R-R-Y. It means 'go quickly'. That book costs thirty shillings. I read ten pages in an hour. [20]

199.   **a. Häve you a péncil?* Dö you häve a péncil? b. Dö you häve súgar in your cöffee?**

With have, *follow either Table 20 or 21 when* have *means* possess. *Follow Table 21 only when* have *is used in other senses. Form questions on pattern (a) or (b) to get the following answers:*

Yes, thank you, I have a cup. No, thank you, no sugar. Yes, please

* *Or, informally,* Have you got a pencil?

TABLE 21

Questions: 'Full' Verbs

Statements	Questions to identify the subject	All Other Questions — Put do or does before the subject, and put the infinitive of the full verb after the subject.
I play the piano.	Who plays the piano? (I do.)	DO I play well?	What DO I play?
We want Robert.	Who wants Robert? (We do.)	DO we want Richard?	Whom (or who) DO we want?
You speak English.	Who speaks English? (You do.)	DO you speak English?	Why DO you speak it?
They catch fish.	Who catches fish? (They do.)	DO they catch fish? DO fishermen catch fish?	Where DO they catch fish?
He plays.	Who plays? (He does).	DOES he PLAY?	What DOES he play?
It hurts.	What hurts? (That does.)	DOES it HURT? DOES the injection HURT?	Whom (or who) does it HURT?
He tries.	Who tries? (He does.)	DOES he TRY?	How DOES he TRY?
She sings.	Who sings? (She does.)	DOES she SING?	When DOES she SING?

99

plenty of milk. Yes, I have some writing paper. No, I have no envelopes. Yes, here are the tickets. I have my bath in the morning, not at night. Yes, I have a bad cold.

200. **Whïch is bïgger, the sún or the mòon? The sùn ïs.**
Whö can änswer this quèstion? Ï cän.
Whät flöats in wàter? Wòod döes.

Using these patterns form questions and answers to them from the following statements.

(*a*) Charles is away today. (*b*) Doüglas (10, 12) and Rälph are àlso awäy. (*c*) Frank knows where they live. (*d*) Hënry and Dönald (6) lïve nëxt dòor to them. (*e*) We must äll dö our bèst. (*f*) Ëxercise is gòod for us. (*g*) Föod këeps us alîve. (*h*) Yöur car göes fäster than mìne. (*i*) Yöurs has a bëtter èngine. (*j*) Ï have a späre kèy. (*k*) You are right. (*l*) Thïs word is wrong.

Indirect questions

201.

Direct	**Indirect**
a. **Whö ìs it?**	**I dön't knöw whò it ïs.**
b. **Häve you a máp?**	**I wönder if you have a màp.**
c. **Äre you rëally enjöying yoursëlf?**	**Äsk him whëther he is rëally enjòying himsëlf.**

In statements in English the subject normally comes before the verb. In the 'other questions' in Table 20, the verb comes before the subject: in other words, we have inversion of the subject and the verb. In the 'other questions' in Table 21, the auxiliary do *precedes the subject. In indirect questions, as in the examples at the beginning of this exercise we return to the normal order, subject and verb. Notice that the question in example (a) does not require the answer* Yes *or* No; *in example (b) the questioner expects a clear answer* Yes (or No); *in example (c) the questioner feels that the answer is in doubt. Form indirect questions beginning with the words in the right-hand column:*

(*a*) Where are we? I have no idea.
(*b*) How are you today? Tell me.
(*c*) Are you better? Everyone is asking.
(*d*) Do you want something to eat? Tell the nurse.
(*e*) How high is that mountain? I wonder.
(*f*) How far is it to the top? Ask the guide.
(*g*) Is there a good view? Who knows.
(*h*) Can we get back before supper? I doubt (it).
(*i*) Whose camera is that? Does anyone know?
(*j*) Does anyone want this old camera? It is hardly worth asking.

TABLE 22
The Negative
Auxiliary and Modal Verbs

Formal or emphatic	Informal		Negative—Interrogative*	
	either	*or*	*Informal*	*Formal or emphatic*
I AM NOT ...	I'm not ...	—	AREN'T I ...?	AM I NOT ...?
You are not ...	You're not ...	You aren't ...	Aren't you ...?	Are you not ...?
He is not ...	He's not ...	He isn't ...	Isn't he ...?	Is he not ...?
We are not ...	We're not ...	We aren't ...	Aren't we ...?	Are we not ...?
They are not ...	They're not ...	They aren't ...	Aren't they ...?	Are they not ...?
My brother is not ...	My brother's not ...	My brother isn't ...	Isn't my brother ...?	Is my brother not ...?
I HAVE NOT ...	I've not ...	I haven't ...	HAVEN'T I ...?	HAVE I NOT ...?
He has not ...	He's not ...	He hasn't ...	Hasn't he ...?	Has he not ...?
I CANNOT ...	I CAN'T (5) ...		CAN'T I ...?	CAN I NOT ...?
I MUST NOT ...	I mustn't (*t silent*) ...		Mustn't I ...?	MUST I NOT ...?

Imperative. Formal. Do not be ... Do not have ...
Informal. Don't be ... etc. *Emphatic:* Don't you be ... etc. Can *and* must *have no imperative.*

* *Examples of the Negative Interrogative:*
(a) Why aren't you réady? (i.e. You're not ready. Why?)
(b) Isn't it 8 o'clock yét? (i.e. It isn't 8 o'clock—time is passing slowly.)
(c) Isn't it 8 o'clóck? (I think it is.)
(d) Isn't it hót today! (It is very hot!)

101

TABLE 23

The Negative

Full Verbs

I DO NOT (run)	I DON'T (17) (run)	DON'T I (run)?	DO I NOT (run)?
HE DOES NOT (run)	HE DOESN'T (run)	DOESN'T he (run)?	DOES HE NOT (run)?

Imperative: Do not run. Don't run. Don't you run.

202. *Put into the negative, then into the negative-interrogative (formal):*

I am the Chairman.* You are a member of the Committee. She is the Secretary. They are all càndidates. This is in order. I can explain. We must speak for ourselves. We know it. He änswers lëtters règularly. The Committee agrees. [10]

(*informal: give two forms when possible*)

I'm good enough. It's working. You're looking smart. The news is bad. You can tell me. I must look. I believe it. That man drives fast. That man's a fast driver. This engine runs smoothly.

203.   **Ïs he älways ríght? He is nòt älways rïght.**
       Döes he öften compláin? He does nòt öften compläin.

Put 185 into the interrogative, and then into the negative, with a suitable adverb of degree or relative time.

Do

204.   **What are you doing? I'm working. I'm mäking a càrd ïndex.**
       What do you do after supper? Sometimes I play cards.

Answer the question What are you doing? (*or* What am I doing? *or* What is — doing?) *20 times, when emphasis falls on action in progress (see 194 a). Then answer the question* What do you do? (*or* What do I do? *or* What does — do?) *20 times with the following adverbial expressions to express the idea in 189 (c):*

in the morning, after breakfast, in the afternoon, in the evening, at night, on Sundays, on Mondays, at Christmas, in the holidays, at the office, in a library, in a shop.

* *Use a capital letter for* Chairman, Committee, *etc. when referring to a specific example.*

205.　　　I wàlk höme (I dön't rùn, | or gö by càr).
　　　　　I dò wälk | — you säy I dön't, but I dò.

Use do (*a*) *for emphasis* (I dò wälk), *to make an affirmative statement in contrast to a negative one; and* (*b*) *to avoid repeating another verb* (You säy I dön't but I dò). *Read and study the following dialogue, filling in the gaps:*

A	B
I play the violin.	Sö do Ì, (i.e. I dö tòo.)
You write exactly like John.	Why, sö I dò! (What a surprìse!)
Your writing's just like his.	Why, sö it ìs! (You're right.)
You must try to write as John does.	But sö I dò. (Thät is whät I dö alrèady.)
You look tired.	— — — (You do too).
It's snowing.	— — — — (What a surprise!)
We wear gloves in winter.	— — — (We do too.)
George wears a scarf.	— — — (John — too.)
John must wear a scarf.	— — — — (That is what he —.)

206.　　**Ĭs Jöhn búsy? I thìnk só. Yës, he ìs.**
　　　　Döes Märy spëak Frénch? I dön't thìnk sö. Nö, she dòesn't.
　　　　Häve you äny móney? I hòpe só. Yès, I hàve.
　　　　Cän you mëet me toníght? I expèct só. Yës, I càn.

Use one of these patterns with each of the following, using a pronoun in the answer.

(*a*)　Is Mr. Jones in?　　　　　(*b*)　Are we late?
(*c*)　Are you all right?　　　　(*d*)　Do you see what I mean?
(*e*)　Can you understand?　　　(*f*)　Is Margaret waiting?
(*g*)　Does she want some tea?　(*h*)　Can you all hear?
(*i*)　Is today Wednesday?　　　(*j*)　Does this coat fit me?
(*k*)　Do bears like hóney (10)?　(*l*)　Can you come to tea today?
(*m*)　Can you find the way?　　(*n*)　Are these questions difficult?
　　　　　　(*o*)　Must we stop now?

207.　　**You äre pléased, áren't you? You ären't àngry, àre you?**
　　　　You täke sùgar, dòn't you? You dön't smóke, dó you?

Repeat first with a rising intonation (asking for the answer yes *or* no*), then with a falling intonation (suggesting you feel sure your statement is true). Then use one of the patterns (and either a falling or rising intonation according to your meaning) with each of the following:*

I am right. He is kind. That isn't cheap. You mean that seriously. You do trust me. Surely you don't believe it. We can see each other

103

sometimes. He plays beautifully. You aren't looking for this magazine. We must take care of our pàrents (19). [10]

208. **I have nö pèn, I have no ink, I have no books. (Räther fòrmal.)**
I häven't a pèn, I haven't any ink, I haven't any books. (Mòre informal*.)

Use both of these patterns in putting the following into the negative:
I have work to do. We have time to spare. I have a car. I have some oil. That child has a coat. This door has a lock. These flowers have water. There is a spare tyre in the boot. There are tools in the toolbox. I am making a complaint. [10]

209. **A single man is one who is not married.**
An orphan is a child who has no father or mother.
A painless operation is one that does not hurt.
Unbreakable glass is glass we cannot break.

Make up sentences, using a verb in the negative, to explain each of the following:

a läzy (13) màn
a blind beggar
a dëaf and dümb chìld
a false statement
different wàys
a nön-smòker
a nön-stöp tràin
unëqual (1) sïdes
undrïnkable wàter
an ïncomplëte ànswer

an impössible quèstion
an immövable òbject
irrëgular vèrbs
ëndless troùble (10)
a forgëtful pèrson
thöughtless pèople
tästeless fòod
a hëlpless ìnvalid
a pöwerless gòvernment
defënceless wòmen   [20]

Negative Prefixes, etc.

210.   **Thïs dësk is üntidy (i.e. not tidy)**

Use the following in sentences of your own: uncertain, uncommon, unhappy, unhealthy, unnatural, unnecessary, unwise, incomplete, ïmpolïte, impossible, irregular, illegal.

211. *Study these two aspects of the negative:*

(a) He does not obey me; i.e. he does not act as I tell him to act.
He disobeys me; i.e.   he acts as I tell him not to act.

* *More informally still.* I haven't got a pen, I haven't got any ink, etc.

(*b*) I put up a ladder,   and take it down; i.e. I revërse the
process.

Men build houses,   and deströy them later.

We do work,   and ündö it àfterwards.

We dress in the morning, and undress at night.

We fasten the door,   and unfasten it next day.

The stars appëar,   and dìsappear.

Passages for Reading, Study and Dictation

212.   Sümmer on a Grëek Ìsland

Ëvery däy and àll dáy, | the sün shïnes döwn fïercely from a clöudless skỳ. We begïn wörk èarly, | with the fïrst mörning lìght, | while it is stïll compäratively còol. By twö o'clóck, | the hëat is sö överpówering | that it is ünwïse to lëave the shäde or dö ánything | excëpt slèep.

To gët to our hŏuse, | we must clïmb a hündred stëep and wïnding (14) stéps | üp from the hàrbour. Our wälls are immënsely thïck and hìgh, | with fëw wïndows, | äll quïte öut of rëach of the gròund. We fästen the dŏor | —ünnëcessarily in thëse dáys— | with hëavy ïron róds | which höok ïnto ïron rïngs in sölid ròck. Insïde, | the wälls of the stäirs are cövered with gúns, swórds* and öther remïnders (14) of wàr.

Yét, | at this móment, | I am sïtting on the térrace, | lòoking at the mòst péaceful scëne you can imàgine. It is gëtting làte, | and the töwn is alrëady in shàdow (4, 17). I am fïrst wríting, thën lòoking at the vïew. To my léft, the läst glöw (17) of sünset is dÿing behïnd the mòuntains on the màinland. A cöol brëeze blöws ïn from the sëa and fäns my chèek. Alöng the närrow päth belŏw me, | a strïng of müles is retürning from some dïstant pärt of the ìsland. The squäre whïte-washed hòuses, lÿing quïetly on the hïll-sídes, | are türning grèy, | and the grëy is grädually dïsappëaring into the därk bàckground. A lïght appèars; | and anòther. Nöw I can önly sëe päle yëllow stärs on a bläck vëlvet cùrtain. A rèal stär, | päle whíte, | shïnes abòve (10).

I gët üp to türn ön my öwn lïght, | but stòp. Behïnd the grëat ròck, | a thòusand fëet hïgh, | on the öther sïde of the tòwn, | the skỳ is gröwing whïter and whïter. I wàtch, | and súddenly | a white flàme bürsts over the skỳ-lïne. Surprïsingly quíckly, | hälf a mŏon, | thrëe-quàrters of a móon, | the füll möon itsèlf rïses. It rësts for a mòment, | äfter its clïmb, | on the hìll-top; then detáches itsëlf, | flöating like a ballöon in the àir.

* sword (7)—w *silent*.

The chürch clöck strìkes. Óne, twó—it is strïking èight. I smell frësh fïsh cöoking on chàrcoal, | and fëel hùngry.

213.   Tea

Tëa is not sïmply an òrdinary drïnk. It is a mätter of táste and cèremony.* Chöose göod tèa-leaves | —gréen, brówn or bláck, as you lïke— | and këep them in an äir-tight contàiner, | prëferably in a tìn. Pöur (20) püre (y, 21) frësh wáter into a clëan kèttle, | nöt into a säucepan whëre you cöok àny kïnd of föod. Mäke süre the tëa-pot is èmpty, | clëan and drỳ. Mäke cërtain that nöne of these utënsils have the hörrible täste of söap or detèrgent.

Püt the kéttle on, | fìrst. Wärm the pòt. Këep it wärm and drỳ. Püt the tèa-leaves ïn. Püt ïn öne téaspoonful | for ëvery twö cüps of tèa. Höw füll must the tëaspoons bè? Thät depënds on your tàste, | and on the strëngth of the tèa. Këep the pöt besïde the kèttle. As söon as the wäter is rëally bóiling, | and whïle it is stíll böiling, | pöur a lïttle ön to the tèa-leaves. Püt the lïd on the tëa-pot and waìt a möment. Then ädd möre of the böiling wäter untïl the pöt contäins as múch as you nèed. Wäit föur or fïve mínutes, | but këep the pöt hòt.

Nöw the tëa is rèady. Söme people drïnk it äs it ìs; | söme with lémon, or súgar, or bòth; öthers with mílk, or sùgar, or bòth. In any cäse, there is nöthing lïke a göod cüp of tèa.

TESTS

214. *Fill each gap with a suitable word, counting* don't, *etc. as one word:*

(*a*) I see, you see, he —; they go, she —; I do, he —; you say, he —: they can, she —; I dress, he —; we must, he —; I have, he —; we try, she —, he doesn't —.

(*b*) Where is the door? There — —. And the stairs? There — —. Shut the door; shut — quietly. Climb the stairs; climb — slowly. Listen to the speaker; listen to —; — — very interesting. Listen to the bells; listen to —; — — unusually clear this evening.

(*c*) Please — quiet. Move —. — make such a noise. I can — hear myself speak.

(*d*) He speaks very good English. He speaks English — —. He has a careful pronunciation. He — his words —. But he is too quick. He speaks — —.

(*e*) (advice, advise, practice, practise) What must I do? What is

* *cèremony:* four syllables (3, 2, 12, 2).

your —? What do you —? You must —. Do an hour's — every evening.

(*f*) (lie *or* lay) Don't — on the wet floor. Get up. — your head on this cushion.

(*g*) That picture is not — —. Can you — (rise *or* raise) it?

(*h*) (say *or* tell). — me, how do you — this in English? Can you — me the time?

(*i*) (do *or* make). You — too many mistakes. You must — better than that.

(*j*) (show *or* explain). Please — me how to do this work. — me. Please — this word to me. — it. [50]

215. **I do not see myself as others see me.**

Repeat this sentence beginning with "you do not see yourself . . . ; *then with* he, she, we, you (*plural*) *and* they.

216. *Answer each question with a complete sentence:*

(*a*) What are you doing at this moment? (*b*) Are you reading a novel? (*c*) Do you understand what you are reading? (*d*) Where do you come from? (*e*) What are you sitting on? (*f*) Can you tell me the weight of the sun? (*g*) How often do you have an English lesson? (*h*) Are you making good progress? (*i*) Do you always correct your mistakes? (*j*) Are you trying to answer this question correctly? [10]

217. *Put the following sentences into the interrogative:*

(*a*) You're tired. (*b*) You need a rest. (*c*) You can go to sleep. (*d*) The guests are here already. (*e*) There is no one to receive them. (*f*) You have a bath every day. (*g*) I have a towel. (*h*) The bath's getting cold. (*i*) It holds a lot of water. (*j*) You advise me to wait.

218. *Form 3 questions for each of the following answers:*

(*a*) George is working in a factory. (*b*) He must earn some money this week. (*c*) John drives a car carefully. (*d*) Jane types her own letters. (*e*) There is too much traffic in the town. (*f*) I can go to the concert tomorrow night. (*g*) Ice melts slowly in winter. (*h*) The days are longer than the nights in summer. (*i*) I have a pain in my back. (*j*) We have an English lesson every day. [30]

219. *Put the sentences below into the negative:*

(*a*) (*formal*). Please apòlogise! I understand. A worker works for nothing. He can live on air. A vòluntary worker expects payment. He

107

is interested in profit. Does he deserve a reward? You realise the difficulties. There are very many. I have something to say. [10]

(b) (*informal*). Drop that vase! It's raining. I think so. Do you want some cake? I have a plate. We have chicken for dinner every day. We can wait. You must be impatient. You look well. I'm feeling very well. [10]

220.   *Arrange the following groups of words so as to form a complete sentence with the proper word-order:*

(a) you, very, well, English, speak.

(b) the moon, can, we, see, very, sometimes, clearly.

(c) I, hardly, that, question, myself, answer, can.

(d) that, sense, sentence, make, not, does, quite.

(e) What, you, in, the holidays, do, do?

(f) in the summer, to the sea, we go, usually.

(g) Who, his friends, sends, good wishes, at Christmas?

(h) You, not, are writing, that, enough, carefully.

(i) We, no, have, often, lessons, on Saturday.

(j) strangers, your private business, do not tell. [10]

5. RELATIONS IN SPACE AND TIME:
POSITION AND DIRECTION

Prëposìtions

221. (*a*) *PRËPOSÏTIONS, like* to, at, from, *exprëss compärative posïtions in späce and tìme. They often express*

$\longrightarrow$ mövement in óne dirëction

$\longleftarrow$ mövement in the óppositè dirëction

$\circ$ mövement in nò dirëction, or nö mövement at àll.

We can consider movement in relation to something which we imagine as having no dimension, or unspecified dimension, i.e. a point in space or time; or as something with one dimension, i.e. a line; with two dimensions, i.e. a surface; or with three dimensions, i.e. a space.

(*b*) *A preposition stands before and 'governs' a noun, noun-group* (see 94) *or pronoun; and nothing can stand between the preposition and what it governs. 'Governs' in this sense means 'express some relationship with the thing referred to'.*

(*c*) *Certain verbs express movement from one place to another, e.g.* come, go, walk, run, bring, send, *and such verbs are therefore associated with prepositions which indicate movement. Other verbs suggest no movement from place to place, e.g.* stay, wait, live, stand, sit, lie, *and such verbs are associated with prepositions which do not indicate movement.*

222. *Study Table 24 and refer to it often.*

Relätions (13) in Späce

Mövement from pläce to pláce, | or nò mövement from pläce to pläce.

223.   **Gö to the dòor. Wäit at the dòor.**

Fill each gap with to *or* at:

(*a*) Come — my room.   (*b*) Run — the gate.   (*c*) Stand — the gate. (*d*) Sit — the table.   (*e*) I must send this — my lawyer.   (*f*) He is waiting — his office for it.   (*g*) Bring the answer — my house. (*h*) We buy sugar — the grocer's.   (*i*) The grocer sells sugar — his shop.   (*j*) He sells it — his cùstomers. [10]

109

TABLE 24

Prepositions

Relations in Space

AS FAR AS a PLACE;   TILL (or UNTIL) a TIME

to, at, from

224.   Come to this spot. Go to the window. Gïve thät to mè.
        This road leads to the fròntier.

110

TO *ïndicates mòvement approaching a pòint, a place (i.e. a point on a map), a person or thing, or a line. Note:* Go home.

Wait at this spot. Meet me at the airport.

At ïndicates no mòvement in relation to a point of place. Note: Stay at home.

A river runs from the mountains to the sea.
It flows away from the mountains.

From *indicates movement, the opposite of approaching; or separation.*
The idea of separation is often strengthened by the use of away *before* from, *especially when* to *is omitted.*

225. *Supply* to, at *or* from:

(a) You can change your money — any bank. Why not go — the bank now?

(b) Send this parcel — my house. I live — number 30.

(c) My car is — the door. Take it — the garage.

(d) Take that knife away — him and bring it — me.

(e) How far is it — here — the next 'bus stop?

(f) Many visitors come — our town and stay — the Grand Hotel.

(g) This road leads — the coast. It ends — Ashton.

(h) I am sitting — my desk, writing a letter — Cècil.

(i) We escape — danger, or others rescue us — it.

(j) We spend the week-end — home and return — work on Monday. [20]

226. *With* speak, talk, listen, belong, *we are interested in the direction of the action and use* to; *with* arrive, look, aim, shoot, laugh, shout, *we are interested in the final point of the action and use* at. *With* point *and* throw *we can use either* to *or* at *according to where we want to put the emphasis. Supply* to *or* at:

(a) Look — me and listen — what I am saying.

(b) Give that — me. It doesn't belong — you.

(c) A train travels from place — place and arrives — its destination.

(d) Throw the ball — Jane, but don't throw it — her.

(e) A compass needle points — the north. We aim — a target.

(*f*) Don't point — other people. Don't laugh — them, and never shout — them.

(*g*) I walk — work and arrive — my office at nine o'clock. [15]

on, off; in, into, out of, outside

227.　**Put your book on the table. Don't run on the flòwer-bëds.**
Sit on the grass, on the side of the road. I am on my way home.

On *indicates movement approaching a surface; or movement or rest when an object has reached a surface or a line, and is supported by it.*

Hëlp me lïft this hëavy bóx | ön to the chàir.

On to *emphasises the idea of movement ending on a surface, or the effort of making that movement.*

Take your feet off the chair.
We're not on the right road—we're a löng wäy òff it.

Off *indicates movement, the opposite of approaching; or separation.*

Now put your book in the drawer. Don't run in school.
Stay in your class-room. *Note:* **Write in English.**

In *indicates movement entering a space; or movement or rest when an object has entered a space and is enclosed by its limits.*

Run into the shelter, then lie flat.

Into *emphasises the idea of movement entering a space.*

Take your book out of the drawer again.

Out of, *movement, the opposite of entering.*

There is a telephone box outside our post-office.
There are also three telephones inside the building,
but you can only use them when the post-office is open.

Öutsìde = not in; **ìnsìde** = not outside.

228. *Supply* on, on to, off, in, into, out of, inside *or* outside:

(*a*) Put this — the floor, — the chair, — your pocket, — your head, — the cupboard, — the kitchen, — the terrace, — the glass, — the wall.

(*b*) Take it — the floor, — the chair (*continue as in* (*a*)).

(*c*) We swim — water; a ship floats — the sea; an aeroplane flies — the air; we ride — horse-back, and ride — a 'bus.

(*d*) You can easily jump — a hole, but you can't jump — it so easily. You can easily fall — a roof, but you can't climb — it so easily.

(*e*) It is freezing — the house. It is much warmer — it. Come — the hall. [30]

229. (*See* 227) *Put* into *or* on to *whenever possible in the following examples; otherwise* in *or* on:

Stand — the platform. Step — the ladder. Dive — the pool. Drive — the town. He is asleep — bed. Slip — bed. Take a seat (i.e. sit down) — the waiting-room. Take these papers — the waiting-room. Help me lift this box — the kitchen, and that one — the roof. [10]

230. *Fill the gap with* at *when you are thinking of a place or a point on the map,* on *when you are thinking specially of a surface,* in *when you are thinking specially of a space or area. Say:* at the beginning, at the end, in the middle.

(*a*) A train arrives — a station. Our friends arrive — the platform. We arrive — the city. A plane arrives — an airport. The plane starts from Páris (4), calls — Beirút (13, 9), and stops — Hongkong.

(*b*) I was born — Wimbledon. I live — Greece. My brother lives — London.

(*c*) There are three buttons — my coat, and a handkerchief — my pocket.

(*d*) — table, we sit — a chair. After lunch Mother rests — an armchair and goes to sleep.

(*e*) — many countries, all children go to school. They stay — school until they are 14 or 15.

(*f*) It is raining hard; we must stay — school today.

(*g*) When we read a book, we start — the beginning. We don't stop — the middle, we finish it — the end. [20]

by, alòng, acròss, through

231. I pass by your house on my way to work. I go past it. Come and sit by me (*or* besìde me). Let's walk along by the river.

By *indicates movement passing a person, place or thing; or either movement or no movement at the side of a person or thing.*
Past *emphasises the latter part of the by movement and means 'by and farther than' the thing referred to.*
Beside *emphasises the idea of 'at the side of'.*

Imägine a ràilway lïne | rünning alöng the cóast, |
göing acröss a ríver, | then acröss a wïde pláin, |
throügh a dëep fórest | and throügh a löng tùnnel.

Alòng, *movement following a line;*
Acròss, *movement from one side of a line or surface to the other, at the same level;*
Through, *movement into and then out of a space.*

232. *Fill the gap with* by, past, along, across *or* through:

On my way home, I walk a hundred yards — the street, go — a wide ávenue (3), — the muséum,* into the park, right — the park, — the gate at the other side, — the bank of the river and — the river to the other side. I pass — some old trees, walk — a narrow path — the railway line, and then take a train. [10]

up, down; with, without, against; between, among, etc.

233. **Up, down,** *e.g.* We climb up a hill. If we are not careful, we slide down a slippery slope.

With *indicates movement in the same direction as something else, accòmpanying (10) it; e.g.*
Please come with me, I don't want to go alone.
The alphabet starts with A and ends with Z.
Join forces with us.
But note: fight with, quarrel with, argue with.

Withòut *indicates that one thing is not accompanied by another; e.g.*
I don't want to go without you.

Agàinst *indicates movement in opposite directions, so that two forces meet in òppositïon; e.g.*
I can't swim against the current. Don't lean against the glass.

* y + 8, 1.

114

Òver, *movement or no movement; e.g.*

We have a roof over our heads to cover us.

A horse can jump over a fence.

Ünder, ündernèath: *movement or no movement; e.g.*

It's raining—but I am shëltering ünder my umbrèlla; *i.e.* my umbrella covers me. It's raining hard—get right underneath the umbrella.

Round (or **aròund**), *e.g.*

I wear a belt round my waist, and a collar round my neck.

My house is just round the corner.

About, *movement or no movement, suggests* 'on all sides', 'in different places'; *e.g.*

The world about us.

Betwèen (two), *movement or no movement; e.g.*

My desk is between the door and the window.

Choose between life and death. Divïde this möney betwèen you (*two*).

Amòng (10) (more than two). Share it among you (*more than two*).

234.   Other relationships in space

For *indicates the öbject or pùrpose of the* to *movement; e.g.*

This train is going to Istanbul: it is the train for Istanbul.

I am giving this present to you: it is for you. I'm sorry for you.

We ask (call, care, hope, long, look, send, wait) for something.

Note: What are you doing that for? *i.e.* Why are you doing it? For what purpose? What is this thing for?

Towàrds (7) *indicates movement in the direction of a point; e.g.*

Be careful—there is a car coming straight towards us.

As far as *emphasises the extent of a movement; e.g.*

Walk with me as far as the end of this road.

In front of; behìnd (14); *e.g.*

There is a small garden in front of our house, and a larger one behind it.

Òpposite; *e.g.*

I am on this side of the table, you are on the opposite side. You are opposite me.

Near, *i.e. at a short distance from a place; e.g.*

Our house is near the sea. Yours is nearer the town.

Next to, *i.e. nearest to, the nearest thing to; e.g.*

I don't like rough wool next to my skin.

Beyònd, *to or at a farther point.*

Don't go too far: don't go beyond your limits.

Abòve (10), *i.e. at a higher lèvel* (3); *e.g.*

Keep your head above the water.

Belòw (17), *i.e. at a lower level; e.g.*

It is very cold—ten degrees belöw frèezing pöint.

235. *Fill each gap with one of the prepositions from 233 or 234.* (*A 'preposition' may consist of two or three words*):

(*a*) My brother and I work well togèther. He works well — me, and I can't work — him.   (*b*) He and I divide the work — us, though sometimes we divide it — several people.   (*c*) In these days, people often travel — the world.   (*d*) We can fly from London to Tokyo — the North Pole.   (*e*) In stormy weather, aeroplanes fly — the clouds.   (*f*) It is a long way to Rome. We cannot walk — Rome; but we can go some way — it.   (*g*) There is a train leaving — Rome soon.   (*h*) The train goes farther than Rome. It goes — it.   (*i*) When we read, we hold the book — us.   (*j*) The back of the chair is — us, and the floor is — our feet.   (*k*) The chair and the floor provïde us — support.   (*l*) Ask — what you want, and hope — the best.   (*m*) I can't find my purse. I am still looking — it.   (*n*) In football, two teams play — each other. The rëferëe (3, 12, 1) warns them — foul play. [20]

Relations in time

236. *Study Table 25 and note the following examples:*

to, till (or until)

The lïbrary (14) is open from 9 to 5 (or from 9 till 5). It is open till 5. *Use* till *when* from *is omitted.* The librärian (19) stays till 6. *The activity continues through a period ending at that time.*

from, since

The library is open from 9 daily. *Use* from *although* to *is omitted.* It has been open daily since 1946. *Use* since *to mean 'through a period starting at that time in the past'.*

TABLE 25

Prepositions: Relationships in Time

T = a point or period of time

FOR *expresses the relationship between an activity and the time it lasts.*

---

before, by, till

We cannot start our journey before 5 (*i.e.* earlier than 5). It's too dark before then.

But we must be on our way by 6 (*i.e. in the progress of time ending not later than then*).

We shall not arrive till 7 this evening. (*Our journey will end then.*)

Certainly, we shall not be there by 6. (*We shall arrive after 6.*)

after, past

If we arrive after 8 (*i.e. if our arrival takes place later than* 8) all the hotels will be full.

It is now half-past 11, past my usual bedtime (*i.e. time, in its progress, has gone beyond 11, etc.*).

at, on, in

The library opens at 9 on every day of the year, except on Sunday.*
It is open in the day-time, in the morning, in the afternoon, in the evening, in spring, in summer, in autumn, in winter; in January, in February, etc. It was opened to the public in 1946, on March 14th.

* On *is frequently omitted*, e.g. the library is open every day except Sunday.

It is closed at night, at Christmas (*or* on Christmas Day), at New Year (*or* on New Year's Day) and at Easter. It was opened on the morning of March 14th.

in, during, through

Do you ever wake up in the night? (*i.e. at some point in that period*)
Do you ever wake up during the night? (*i.e. while the night is progressing*)
Yes, I often lie awake during the night. (*Here the activity of lying awake is also progressing.*)
Some people sleep right through the night. (*From one end of the period to the other.*)

for

(*a*) I sleep for eight hours every night. (*My sleep lasts that time.*)
(*b*) I have been ill for a fortnight. (*My illness has lasted that time.*)
(*c*) I will be away for three weeks. (*My absence will last that time.*)
N.B. *You may omit* for *in these examples.*

for, before

We shall not arrive before 6 o'clock.
It is now 4 and we shall not arrive for two hours. (*Do not omit* for *in this case.*)

for, in, within

My father walks for half an hour every morning. (*His walking lasts that time.*)
He walks to his office in twenty minutes. (*His walk to the office is completed by the end of that period.*)
I can walk that distance within twenty minutes easily (*i.e. inside the limits of that period*).
John will be home in five minutes (*i.e. at the end of a period lasting 5 minutes from now*).

237. *Fill each gap with one of the prepositions from 236:*

(*a*) I was born — five o'clock — the morning, — February 3rd. I have lived here — 1956.
(*b*) I was born — the morning of February 3rd, — winter.
(*c*) The sun shines — the day-time, the stars shine — night.
(*d*) Tuesday comes — Monday and — Wednesday.
(*e*) I go to bed — ten, sleep — six, or half — six. I never wake up — the night, but sleep right — it.
(*f*) We start work — eight — the morning — the summer, and finish — one, except — Saturday, when we work — half — twelve.

118

(g) I study — three hours every day — October — April. So I study — the autumn and all — the winter.

(h) Go on working — lunch-time. Finish this exercise — then. If you finish it — then, start the next. In any case, work quietly — the next hour.

(i) Mr. Taylor is out. He will be back — a quarter of an hour.

(j) Can you keep your head under water — two minutes?

(k) I want to buy some food. The shop closes — 6. So I must get there — 6. I cannot get there — 5.30 but that gives me enough time.

(l) We started learning English — 1966. It is now 1968. We have been learning it — 1966, — two years.

(m) We shall go on studying it — a long time yet. [40]

Relationships of a more abstract kind

238. **Of** *.

We get coal from the earth. Bricks are made of earth or clay.

(a) *While* from *expresses the idea of physical movement or separation*, of *expresses a relationship of a more general or abstract kind.*

(b) Of *expresses the relationship between a part and the whole, a member and the whole body, a quality and the thing possessing it; e.g.* A quarter of an hour, the cause (7) of the accident, the effèct of it; a member of a society (12, 22, 2), the heat of the sun.

(c) Of *indicates* **rëference** *to something in thought or speech; e.g.* Think of a number. We are thinking of you (*i.e.* you are in our thoughts). We were speaking of George (*i.e.* refèrring to him). What do you think of Kàtherine? (*i.e.* What is your opinion of her?) Everyone speaks well of her.

About *indicates general treatment of the subject-matter of thought, e.g.* A book about bees. Think about your work, don't talk about it. We know (speak, ask, write, agree, worry, dream, care) about something.

On *indicates a more exact treatment of the subject-matter; e.g.* A book (a lecture) on the physïcal effëcts of spàce trävel. Can we now agree on a dëfinite propósal (17)?

By *indicates the agent or means by which something is done or produced; e.g.* A book by a fämous (13) aùthor. Made by hand. Travel by train. Häppen by chànce.

* *Pronounce* of *as* [ov].

119

With *indicates the ïnstrument or mànner; e.g.*
Write with a pen, with care. (*See also 233.*)

For *indicates exchànge; e.g.*
How much do you pay for a new pair of shoes? Thank you for your kind attention.

Like *indicates comparison; e.g.*
Open the window. This room is like an oven. It is more like a Turkish bath. A noise like thunder. He runs like lightning.

As (*i.e. in the capacity of*); *e.g.* He acts as a father to me.

Excèpt; *e.g.* Everyone is ready except you.

Instèad (3) **of;** *e.g.* I don't want to go to the concert. Ÿou go instèad of me.

239. *Fill each gap with one of the prepositions from 238:*

(*a*) Today, we can travel — road, — rail, — sea, — air. We can still go on foot or on horseback. A train works — steam, — electrìcity, or — dìesel (1) ëngine. Evënts öften häppen — àccident.

(*b*) Workmen work — tools. Döctors perförm öperätions — ìnstruments. In these days, people no longer fight — bows and arrows, but they still fight — one another.

(*c*) I know a little — wild flowers, but I want a good book — the subject — a real expert. Can I change this book — another one? In other words, can I have another — this one?

(*d*) Scïentists discüss their sübject with öne anòther. They ärgue — it, and sömetimes agrèe — it, but they sëldom agrëe — a fïnal (14) ànswer.

(*e*) I often think — (*i.e.* remember) your family. Tell me — them. Do you get letters — them? What do they think — your discòvery? Will you get any reward — it?

(*f*) Give me three gallons — petrol, please, — the red pump.

(*g*) What are these chairs made — ? A special wood that comes — South America. Each set — chairs is made — one tree. They are all made — hand.

(*h*) There is a good view — the town — the hill, and a good view — the hill — my window.

(*i*) I dön't emplöy a làwyer. My bròther äcts — my läwyer. Howèver, he doesn't write — a lawyer: he doesn't use long words.

(*j*) John travels half rate, — a student. He doesn't always look — a student: he is too tidy. [40]

Some special cases

240. (a) *Prepositions after verbs:*

We *accüse* pëople *of* döing wròng.
We *appröve* (9) *of* whät is rìght.
We *belïeve in* the pëople we trùst. We häve *fàith in* them.
We often *blame* others *for* our own faults (7).
We *call on* people when we visit them.
The police *charge* wrongdoers *with* their crimes.
We *compare* one thing *with* (*or to*) another.
I *congrätulate* you *on* your succèss.
Cover these things *with* a cloth. They are *covered with* dust.
Lët us fïrst *decïde on* whät we wànt. Thät *depènds on* whät there ìs.
Fill this bottle *with* water. It is now *full of* water.
Forgïve me *for* interrùpting. I don't want to *ïnterfère with* you—I
mean *interfere in* your discussion: but may I *join ín* it?

(b) *—after adjectives:*

We are *afräid of* the dárk, *ashämed of* our wéakness, nöt älways
cërtain of the trúth, *fönd of* pléasure, *füll of* stränge idëas and ím-
pulses, *guïlty of* mäny érrors, *jëalous* (3) *of* öther pëople's succéss and
nöt älways *süre of* succèss oursèlves. We can get *rid of* some of these
faults, but not all of them. Each one of us is *different from* his neigh-
bour, and each is *interested in* himself. We wänt to be *fämous for*
sòmething. Are you *tired of* this? Then let us go on with the next
subject.

(c) *—after nouns:*

Trÿ to änswer these quèstions: mäke an *attèmpt at* them.
Whät is the *effèct of* a bräke on a machìne?
Whät *ïnfluence* dòes a göod fäther häve *on* his chìldren?
Höw can he këep *contròl over* them?
Dòes he täke *cáre of* them?
Whät is your *opïnion on* (*or about*) cäpital pùnishment?
Häve you äny *ínterest in* this mätter, or any doúbt aboüt it?

241. **Whère are you gòing to? Tö a mèeting.**

*Fill each gap with a suitable preposition. Then answer the question
with a phrase beginning with the same preposition, as in the model.*

(a) Where do you come —?   (b) What are you sitting —?
(c) What are you looking —?   (d) Who is this book —?
   (*this book*)   (*author*)
(e) What is it —? (*subject*)   (f) What language is it —?

(g) What are the words printed —?

(h) What are you talking —?

(i) Who are you talking —?

(j) What do you write —? (*pen*)

(k) What is your pen full —?

(l) Who does it belong —?

(m) What is bread made —?

(n) Where do we get flour —?

(o) What do we use bread —?

(p) What do we cut bread —?

(q) What are you afraid —?

(r) What are you laughing —?

(s) What are you waiting —?

(t) What are you listening —?

(u) Who is the present —? (*sender*)

(v) Who is it —? (*receiver*)

(w) Which room do you work —?

(x) Which desk do you sit —?

(y) What condition is your book —?

(z) What letter does the alphabet end —?

Test using various prepositions

242. *Fill each gap with a suitable preposition. (A 'preposition' may consist of more than one word.)*

(a) I must call — the Mayor,* then get my ticket — the trável ägency (13), and then go — the bank. My appöintment — the Mayor is — ten minutes. Can you call — a taxi?

(b) There is no need — a taxi. The Mayor's office is only — the corner. The travel agency is — this side — it, the bank is — the other. The Mayor's office is — the travel agency and the bank. — other words, the bank is just — his office.

(c) — the bank, we can go straight — the street — the library. The library is therefore — bank. It is open — four hours — the morning, — nine — one, every day — Sunday. — the afternoon it is open — six, but not — Saturday.

(d) Now walk — me — the university. Or is that too far? Then come — the next cross-roads.

(e) I have a better idea. — that, let's have a drink — this cafe. We'll sit — this table. Tell me — your family. How much do I owe — two cups of coffee?

(f) Thank you — the drink. There's nothing — a good cup — coffee.

(g) John, you've done very well. I congrätulate you — süch a succéssful resùlt. I'm very proud — you. But you haven't much influence — your brother.

(h) George, I must be hònest — you. I am not happy — your work.

* *Pronounce as* [mare].

It is full — mistàkes. You dön't täke enoügh ìnterest — it. I höpe you're ashàmed — yoursëlf.

(i) Jane, there's no doubt — it. You have mèasles. You're covered — spots. You must stay — bed and we'll send — the doctor. Take care — yourself.

(j) People need a roof — their heads, and firm ground — their feet. A swimmer must keep his head — the surface — the water: a diver must not go too far — it. How can a diver stay — the water — air? And how can he get — his suit?

(k) Where is the nearest hòspital, please? You see that garage, two hundred yards — here? Drive — it, but twenty yards — this side — it, turn right. The hospital is then a hundred yards — the road — your left. It's on a hill. Drive — the gate and — the slope.

(l) I don't want to quarrel — George. I'm very fond — him. I can't blame him — being what he is. I am, after all, respònsible — him. But we can't always combïne büsiness — plèasure. It depënds —cìrcumstances.

(m) Shakespeare was born — Stratford, — 1564, — Saint George's Day. He lived — 52 years, — 1616.

(n) — many parts — the world, people still draw water — wells. — big cities, they get it — pipes which bring it — the ground — rèservoirs.* Draw a bucket — water — this well. What is the depth — the well?

(o) My opinion — this subject is different — yours. I am afraid I cannot agree — you. Apart — that, I have the greatest respect — your theories, but I think you are mistaking one thing — another. We must think — it again. In any case, can we decide — the date — our next meeting? Good-bye, then, — next Tuesday.

(p) Think — English — your English lesson. — it, remember what you have learnt. [100]

Ädvërbial Pàrticles

243. *Words like* on, off, in, up, down, across, through, *etc. can be used either (a) as prepositions which govern a noun, or pronoun, or (b) as adverbs telling us how or in what direction or position an action takes place. Examples:*

Preposition + Noun or Pronoun	Adverbial Particles
Come into my office.	Cöme ìn.
Stay in your room.	Stäy ìn.
Keep inside the house.	Këep insìde.

* Pronounce—voir (French) as [vwar].

Don't go outside it.	Dön't gö outsìde.
Don't run across the street.	Wàlk acröss.
I pass by your house.	Every day, I päss bỳ.
Imagine you are walking along the road.	You are wälking alòng.
Step on the 'bus.	Stëp ön quìckly.
Jump off it.	Jümp òff agäin.

You may use the following words as prepositions, or as adverbial particles to indicate direction or position: on, off; in, inside, outside; up, down, across, through; over, under; by, along, past. *Do not use* to, at, from, *and* with *as adverbial particles.*

Note these special cases:

Preposition	Adverbial Particle
Go out of the room.	Gö òut.
Stand in front of the class.	Ständ in frònt.
Come away from the fire.	Cöme awày.

And note these adverbial particles:

Keep still: dön't rün abòut (i.e. in any or every direction).
Türn ròund: face the other way.
Türn òver: make the movement in Table 24. $\left(\overset{\curvearrowright}{} \right)$
Dön't gö awày: plëase cöme bàck.

And these uses of adverbial particles:

Is Mr. Smith in? I am sörry, he is òut.
Whät tïme do you gët ùp?
Are you still in bed, or äre you ùp?
There goes the bell—the lësson is òver (finished).
There is no more bread—there isn't any òver (remaining).
Upward(s), downward(s), forward(s), backward(s), *emphasise movement to a higher level, to a lower level, to the front, to the back; e.g.*

This arrow is pointing upwards ⟶ , this is

pointing downwards ↘ , this is pointing

forwards ⟶ , and this backwards ⟵ .

Use after *as a preposition,* afterwards *(i.e. later) as an adverb; before as both. Examples:* Do you read your newspaper before breakfast or after it? I have seen this before. I will see it again afterwards.

Üpstäirs *and* dòwnstäirs* *are adverbial expressions used only with the meaning* 'up, or down, the stairs in a building; on a higher or lower floor'.

244.   **ÈNTER   = CÒME (or GO) ÌN**
         ÈNTRANCE = WÄY ÌN

Enter *means* come (or go) in, *and* an entrance *is a* way in. *The choice is a question of style.* Come in *and* way in *are not only less formal but also more emphatic. In any case, the pattern of simple verb (or noun)* + *particle is very common in English. We often feel that the simple verb needs completion by an adverbial particle. Thus we wake up, pick something up, throw something away.*

245. *Fill each gap with a suitable adverb from 243 and 244:*

(*a*) EXIT means 'way —'. 'Return' means 'go —'. (*b*) The path to the sümmit is the way —. (*c*) We go up the hill and — again. (*d*) We're on the wrong side of the river. How can we get —? (*e*) A fence. How can we get —? A hole in the wall. How can we get —? (*f*) Don't come in here. Stay —. I don't want that. Take it —. (*g*) Let me see the back of your coat. Turn —. (*h*) I can't walk any farther. I must go — now, and lie —. (*i*) Why are you walking — all the time. Sit — and relàx. (*j*) You're sitting on my hat. Get —. (*k*) When prisoners escape, they run —. The police hope to bring them —. (*l*) There is an interesting article in that paper. I want to cut it —. Don't throw it —. (*m*) When you see someone lying badly hurt in the street, do you stop or simply walk —? Do you try to pick him —? (*n*) We are not getting — (*i.e.* making progress). In other words, we're not moving —. On the contrary, we're going —. (*o*) Old Mrs. Jones is in bed. Her room is above us. In other words, she is —, but she is not —. (*p*) There is no food —, so the meal is —. (*q*) Show that to me after the lesson. I want to see it —. (*r*) In which direction is the second arrow pointing in 243? —.

246. **Come to my office. My òffice is üpstàirs. Còme üp to my òffice.**

We often emphasise the direction or position of an action by using this pattern. In the example given, up *is an adverbial particle, to is a preposition.*

Fill the gaps in (*a*) *and* (*b*), *then continue in the same way with the rest of the exercise:*

(*a*) Go to the basement. We are now upstairs. Go — — the basement. (*b*) Go to the post-office. It is on the other side of the street.

* *In isolation, pronounce* üpstàirs; dòwnstàirs.

Go — — the post office. (c) Then go to the bank. It is farther along the street. (d) Then go to the baker's. That is round the corner. (e) Go to the post-office again. It is bäck thère. (f) Put this on the roof. (g) Lay it on the floor. (h) Here is a wall. Jump to the other side. (i) Here is a hole. Crawl to the other side. (j) There is somebody hurt in the road. Don't pass on the other side.

Other uses of adverbial particles

247. **On** *can mean* 'fòrward' (——→); *e.g.* Gö òn (contìnue).

Up *can indicate a stop, e.g.* höld ùp (delay), gïve ùp (surrènder); *or it can indicate aròusal, or the accëleràtion or complëtion of an action, e.g.* Hùrry üp, pläy ùp, ëat ùp.

In *can indicate collapse, e.g.* Give in.

Off *can indicate* 'off or away from a starting line'; *e.g.* Stärt òff (*or* sët òff) on a journey. We are off, *i.e.* we have started.

Out *can suggest a sudden or wide opening; e.g.* Bürst öut làughing. Sprëad òut; *or taking or digging something out of a mass of other things; e.g.* Hëlp me wörk öut the ànswer. Plëase pöint öut my mistàkes. Fïnd öut yöur òwn mistäkes; *or it can suggest disappearance: e.g.* Blöw öut the càndle. The fïre is òut.

248. *Fill each gap with one of the little words from 247:*

(a) Don't stop. Go —. You're holding everyone —.

(b) What is the answer? Don't give —. Work it — for yourself.

(c) Wake —. Hurry — and get — with your breakfast. Eat it —.

(d) I can't talk about it now, I'm just going — to a meeting.

(e) Please point — what we are doing wrong. We can't find —.

(f) You are all too close together. Spread —.

(g) In many countries, maläria (19) is now dying —; and scientists are thinking — höw to prevënt òther disëases.

(h) I can't hear you. Speak —. [15]

249. **Wälk up the hìll. Pïck üp your hàt.**

Pattern A   Wälk |up the hìll.|

Variations {

Wälk |up the hïll| slòwly.

Wälk slòwly |up the hìll.|

Wälk |ùp it.|

Wälk slòwly |üp it.|

126

Pattern B   (i) Pïck üp your hàt. (ii) Pïck your hàt üp.

Variations
Pïck up your hät   Pïck your hät üp at
at ònce.   ònce.

—   Pïck it ùp.

—   Pïck it üp at ònce.

In Pattern A, the verb walk *is intransitive and has no object;* up *is a preposition governing* the hill. *Notice that the preposition is not separated from the noun it governs, and that the adverb,* slowly, *comes either after the verb or after the prepositional phrase. In Pattern B, the verb* pick *is transitive and has an object,* your hat. Up *is a particle indicating the direction in which the action is performed. We might say that the verb is really* pick up. *But notice that the direct object can come either after* pick *or after* pick up. *If the object comes after* pick, *then* up *must come immediately after the object. Notice the position of the adverb* at once. *Notice, also, that if the object is a pronoun,* it, *then* pick it up *is the only possible arrangement.*

250.   *Say whether the sentences below follow Pattern A or Pattern B in 249, or the pattern in 246. If a sentence follows Pattern B* (Pick up your hat) *then give its alternative form* (Pick your hat up):

(*a*) Put on your coat.   (*b*) Take off your hat.
(*c*) Sit on the cushion.   (*d*) Look at the pictures.
(*e*) Work out the answer.   (*f*) Walk out of the room.
(*g*) Walk up the road.   (*h*) Wake up the children.
(*i*) Drink up your tea.   (*j*) Go up into the gallery.
(*k*) Call for the doctor.   (*l*) Call up the doctor (*i.e.* tele-
                                       phone him).

(*m*) Set off on a journey.   (*n*) Put on the kettle.
(*o*) Call on the doctor.   (*p*) Look up the chimney.
(*q*) Look up this word.   (*r*) Give me back my wallet.
(*s*) Take away this rubbish.   (*t*) Take out your books.
(*u*) Write to Margaret.   (*v*) Bring along your friends.
(*w*) Run along the path.   (*x*) Swim across the stream.
                 (*y*) Throw over a rope. [25]

251.   *In 249, there are 4 variations on Pattern A, and 5 on Pattern B. Provide similar variations for the examples in 250. Supply suitable adverbs: you need not choose a different adverb every time.*

127

Passages for Reading and Study.

252.   A Japanese Inn

At last the taxi turns up into a narrow side street and stops outside
a dark wooden building with a lantern above the entrance into[1] a
small courtyard full of shrubs and ferns; it is the *ryokan*, the Japanese
inn, in which I am to spend my first few days in Tokyo. Glass doors
slide back on to[2] an entrance hall a foot or so above the ground;
women wearing kimonos kneel above the step, bowing their foreheads
to the ground in salutation. We remove our shoes and step up on to
the polished wooden floor and slip our feet into slippers which have
neither heels nor backs, and one of the women leads us up steep bare
wooden stairs into a corridor of similarly polished bare boards. There
are sliding screens all down[3] one side and outside some are slippers.
At the end she slides back a screen into[4] a tiny entrance hall, then
slides yet another screen into[4] a room empty of everything except a
low table in the middle. The floor is covered with what looks like
finely woven straw matting. We discard our slippers and step into the
room, on to the *tatami*. We sit on flat cushions on the floor, round the
table.

*Pick out all the prepositions and adverbial particles in this passage
and study the meaning of them in the context. Note the following cases,
marked by numbers in the text:*

1. into: through the entrance, we go *into* a small courtyard.
2. back on to: the doors slide *back*, and are then open; this allows
us to step up *on to* an entrance hall.
3. all down: as we go *down* the corridor, *i.e.* away from our starting point, we see that all of one side consists of sliding screens.
4. into: a screen covers an entrance through which we go *into* an
entrance hall: and another screen covers an entrance through which
we step into a room.

253.   As Others See Us

An African chief, whom I had often met in his native land, came
to England for the first time when he was past sixty. He had never
before left his own country—in which he held a high and responsible
post—and he flew over to London in a few hours, from the home he
knew so well, to a strange and over-crowded city. A friend of mine
went to call on him the morning after his arrival. My friend asked the
chief how he was and whether he was enjoying himself. The visitor
said that he was feeling well, but that he had had a frightening ex-

perience that morning. He had gone, he said, for a walk round the streets and had found himself at Victoria Station. He said 'Naturally, I went in to see your trains. I stood near some iron railings, by an iron gate, to watch a train come in. It was there that I saw this frightening thing.' As the train came nearer and nearer to where I was standing, all the doors at one moment swung outward, and while the train was still moving, a great many men jumped out, quite silently, and began to run towards me. They carried umbrellas like spears, and their faces were set and unsmiling. I thought something terrible was about to happen, so I ran away.'

Well, there it is. There is your business train, the 8.50 or the 9.15 arriving at a London station. And there we are, as this elderly African sees us, on his first day among us.

Pick out all the prepositions and adverbial particles in this passage. Then answer the following questions, beginning each answer with a preposition or a particle, as in the example.

Example: **Where did the chief go to? To England.**

(*a*) Where had the speaker met him before? (*b*) How old was he? (*c*) Where did he fly? (*d*) Where did he fly from? (*e*) Who did the speaker's friend go to call on? (*f*) Where had the chief gone earlier that morning? (*g*) When had he gone for a walk? (*h*) Where did he find himself? (*i*) Where did he go then? (*j*) Where did he stand? (*k*) In which direction did the doors swing? (*l*) In which direction did the men jump? (*m*) In which direction did they begin to run? (*n*) How did they carry their umbrellas? (*o*) On which day did this happen?

6. ACTIVITY SEEN FROM VARIOUS ASPECTS OF TIME

The Ordinary Past Tense

254. **I waited all last week for your letter and only received it yesterday.**

I waited *and* I received *are in the* **Ordinary Past Tense.** *Use this Tense when your point of view is a moment or period in the past separated from the present. An adverb like* yesterday, *or* last week, *shows that the speaker's point of view is in the past.*

The Pre-present Tense

255. **We have climbed a löng wày. We're nearly there.**
I have climbed Füji önce—I don't want to do it again.

We have climbed, I have climbed *are in the* **Pre-present** (*or* **Present Perfect**) **Tense.** *Use this tense when your point of view is the present moment* (*e.g. the time when you say* 'We're nearly there, I don't want') *but when you are looking back to action performed until or before now* (*e.g.* We have climbed). *Our point of view is not at a particular time in the past separated from the present: it is now.*

256. *The Past is a 'simple' Tense. It consists of one word, i.e. a certain form of the verb. The Pre-present is a compound tense, consisting of an auxiliary* (*e.g.* have) *plus a form of the verb called the* **Päst Pàrticiple.** *The Past Tense and the Past Participle of regular verbs have the same form; and this form is the same for every person, singular and plural. In the Pre-present, only the auxiliary changes, as in Table 15.*

Example:

Past Tense	Pre-present
I (you, he, we, they) climbed	I (you, we, they) have climbed
	he has climbed

257. (*See Table 26*) I play   (*1st Person singular, Present Tense*)
                        he plays   (*3rd* ,,   ,,   ,,   ,,)
                        he played (*3rd* ,,   ,,   *Past*   ,,)

Say and spell these three parts of the following regular verbs:

act, advïse, applÿ, attënd, close, clothe, bathe, beg, breathe, brush, call, change, dance, fit, föllow, help, lïsten, own, paint, pass, refër, smoke, süffer, trävel, use, vïsit, walk, wash, watch, wrap. [30]

TABLE 26

Scheme for Forming
the Past Tense and Past Participle
of Regular Verbs

Infinitive ending in	*e.g.*	*Past Tense and Past Participle*	*Note*
Soft sounds (*except*) d	play, call, raise, judge	played, called, raised, judged	*same number of syllables; ending in sound* d
Hard sounds (*except* t)	stop, work, dress, wash, touch, fix	stopped, worked, dressed, washed, touched, fixed	*same number of syllables; ending in sound* t
d *or* t *sound*	mend, want, fade, taste	mended, wanted, faded, tasted	*extra syllable, i.e. id*

Compare this with Table 18

Note: stop, stopped; prefer, preferred; try, tried; raise, raised. (See footnote to 87.)
Exceptions (*in spelling only*)*:* lay, laid (*see* 164); pay, paid.

Irrẽgular Vèrbs

258. *Irregular verbs in common use* (*to which Table 26 does not apply*) *are given in the lists below. Learn their* **principal parts** *in the tradïtional òrder—Infinitive, Past Tense, Past Participle:*

I. *Past Tense and Past Participle ending in* d

Infinitive	*Past Tense*	*Past Participle*
have (4)	had	had
hear (18)	heard (11)	heard (11)
make	made	made
say (13)	said (13)	said (3)
sell	sold	sold
spread (3)	spread (3)	spread (3)
tell	told	told

II. *Past Tense and Past Participle ending in* t

(*a*)   burst   burst   burst
(*like* burst: cost, cut, hit, hurt, let, put, set, shut, split)
(*b*)   bend   bent   bent
(*like* bend: lend, send, spend, build)

131

Infinitive	*Past Tense*	*Past Participle*
(c) burn	burnt	burnt

(like burn: learn, smell (smelt), spell (spelt), spill (spilt), spoil. *These six verbs have regular forms also.)*

(d) (1)	(3)	(3)
bleed	bled	bled
creep	crept	crept
feed	fed	fed
feel	felt	felt
keep	kept	kept
meet	met	met
sleep	slept	slept
sweep	swept	swept
deal	dealt	dealt
dream	dreamt	dreamt
leave	left	left
mean	meant	meant
(e)	(6)	(6)
get	got	got
lose (9)	lost	lost
shoot (9)	shot	shot
(f)	(7)	(7)
bring	brought	brought
buy	bought	bought
fight	fought	fought
think	thought	thought
catch	caught	caught
teach	taught	taught

III. *Past Participle ending in* n

(a) (17)	(9)	(17)
blow	blew	blown
grow	grew	grown
know	knew	known
throw	threw	thrown
also fly (14)	flew	flown
(show, sow, sew—*see footnote*)		
(b) (7)	(9)	(7)
draw	drew	drawn

show, sow and sew—*all three pronounced with vowel* 17—*have regular forms, but the old past participles* shown, sown, *and* sewn (*all vowel* 17) *are still used.*

132

Infinitive	Past Tense	Past Participle
(c) (19)	(7)	(7)
bear	bore	borne
swear	swore	sworn
tear	tore	torn
wear	wore	worn

Mixed

(d) be	was* (6) were* (11)	been
do	did	done (10)
go	went	gone (6), (*or* been, see 265)
lie (*see* 164)	lay	lain

(lie, *meaning* 'tell an untruth', *is regular*)

see	saw	seen
shine	shone (6)	shone (6)

IV. *Past Participle with an extra syllable, ending in* n

(a)	(17)	(17)
freeze	froze	frozen
speak	spoke	spoken
steal	stole	stolen
break (13)	broke	broken
wake	woke	woken†
choose (9)	chose	chosen
(b)	(8)	(13)
shake	shook	shaken
take	took	taken
(c)	(17)	(2)
drive	drove	driven
ride	rode	ridden
rise	rose	risen
write	wrote	written

Mixed

(d)	beat	beaten
beat	beat	beaten
bite	bit	bitten
eat	ate	eaten
fall	fell	fallen
forgët	forgöt	forgòtten
give (2)	gave	given (2)
hide	hid	hidden
tread (3)	trod	trodden

* I **was,** he **was;** you, we, they **were.**   † Regular forms are also used.

133

V. *Vowel change only, without an added* d, t *or* n.

Infinitive	Past Tense	Past Participle
(a)	(3)	(3)
hold	held	held
lead (1)	led	led
read (1)	read (3)	read (3)
(b)	(4)	(10)
begïn	begän	begùn
drink	drank	drunk
ring	rang	rung
sing	sang	sung
sink	sank	sunk
spring	sprang	sprung
swim	swam	swum
run	ran	run
(c)	(10)	(10)
dig	dug	dug
hang	hung*	hung*
stick	stuck	stuck
sting	stung	stung
strike	struck	struck
swing	swung	swung
win	won	won
(d) (14)	(16)	(16)
bind	bound	bound
find	found	found
grind	ground	ground
wind	wound	wound†
(e)		
come (10)	came	come (*see* 265)
sit	sat	sat
stand	stood (8)	stood (8)

259.   Learn the irregular verbs, a group or two at a time. However, you will remember them best by using them in exercises, noticing them in reading, and using them again in conversation and written composition.

* *However, we say* 'Criminals used to be hanged'.
† *Do not confuse this with the regular verbs* wind (2) *and* wound (9).

Interrogative and Negative of Past and Pre-present Tenses

TABLE 27

Past Tense

Interrogative and Negative

I was, you were	Was I? Were you?	I was not.* You were not.*
I had	Had I?	I had not.*
I played	DID I play?	I DID NOT* play.

Contracted forms: I wasn't, you weren't, I hadn't, I didn't play.

260. **He lòoked. Dïd he lóok? Yès, he lòoked. Nò, he dìdn't löok.**
He saw. Did he see? Yes, he saw. No, he didn't see.

Repeat with:

watch	remember	draw	bite	ring
notice	forget	paint	swear	knock
listen	fight	try	arrive	learn
hear	think	succèed	leave	teach
talk	sleep	know [25]	write	buy
speak	climb	understand	telephone	sell
go	fall	dive	ask	steal
come	wake	swim	answer	hide
win	walk	drive	sing	begin
lose	run	ride	drink	end [50]

261. **You älways sàid so. Dïd you ever sáy so? Nö, I nèver säid so.**

Repeat with the first 25 words in Exercise 260, using various adverbs of frequency and adding something suitable, in place of so, *to complete the sentence.*

TABLE 28

Pre-present Tense
Interrogative and Negative

I have bèen	Háve I bëen?	I have nòt* bëen
I have had	Have I had?	I have not had
I have played	Have I played?	I have not played

Contracted form : I hàven't or I've nòt.

262. **I have been (in many places). Have I been (everywhere)? No, I haven't been (everywhere).**

Repeat with first 25 words in Exercise 260, adding something suitable to complete the sentence.

263. **We have älways bëen (sòmewhere). Häve we ëver bëen (hëre befóre)? Nó, | we have nèver bëen (hëre befóre).**

Repeat with the second 25 words in Exercise 260, using various adverbs of frequency, and adding something to complete the sentence.

Choice between Pre-present and Ordinary Past

264. **A. I am wrïting a pòem (17 + 2). Have yoú ever wrïtten a pöem?**

    B. Yës, I hàve. I hàve wrïtten a pöem.

    (*or* Nö, I hàven't. I've nèver wrïtten a pöem.)

    A. When did you write one? B. I wrote one last week.

Make up similar sequences, beginning with the sentences below. Use different expressions of time in place of last week, e.g.

last month, last year, last spring, last summer, last autumn, last winter, the year before last, yesterday, the day before yesterday, two days ago, when I was a child (at school, on holiday).

(*a*) I am rëading a nòvel (6). (*b*) I am making a cake.
(*c*)   doing an expèriment (3). (*d*)   drawing a map of Japàn.
(*e*)   teaching a class. (*f*)   building a wall.
(*g*)   painting a picture. (*h*)   catching cold.
(*i*)   eating a mèlon (3). (*j*)   wearing dark glasses.
(*k*)   very angry with George. (*l*) John drives a car.
(*m*) George rides a bìcycle (14). (*n*) He swims in the river before breakfast.

(*o*) John runs a mile in five minutes. (*p*) He speaks on the radio.

(*q*) Mary is using a typewriter. (*r*) She wants a typewriter of her own.

(*s*) She has found a purse. (*t*) Oh, I trod on a snake.
(*u*) I've bitten my tongue. (*v*) I've torn my finger-nail.
(*w*) I fëll döwnstàirs yësterday. (*y*) I've forgotten my mother's birthday.

(*z*) I've left my book at home.

265.

A. (You are here now).
Where have you been?
Have you ever been $\begin{cases} \text{to Peking?} \\ \text{here before?} \end{cases}$
Yes, I have. I've been $\begin{cases} \text{there once.} \\ \text{here before.} \end{cases}$
When did you $\begin{cases} \text{go there?} \\ \text{come here?} \end{cases}$
I $\begin{cases} \text{went there} \\ \text{came here} \end{cases}$ twenty years ago.

B. George has gone to Mexico.
He has been to Spain.
He went there first.
Now he is in Mexico (or on his way there).

Use been *as the past participle of* go *when the goer has visited a place but is no longer there. Use* been *as the past participle of* come *when referring to a previous visit. Use the two sequences above, A and B, with other subjects (instead of* you *and* George*), other places and other expressions of time.*

266.   a. Öpen the dòor, plëase. I've òpened it. (*Say this after the action is finished.*)

b. Wäsh your hànds. $\begin{cases} \text{But I've wäshed them alrèady.} \\ \text{I've alrëady wàshed them.} \end{cases}$

c. Häve you sëen the néwspaper? Yes, I've jüst sèen it.

d. Has Chárles sëen it yët? No, he hàsn't sëen it yët.

e. Höw lòng have yoü bëen hère? (*i.e. until now*).
I arrived at twelve o'clock. It is now three.
I have been here $\begin{cases} \text{since twelve o'clock.} \\ \text{for three hours.} \end{cases}$
(Since *marks the beginning of the pre-present period. Use* for *when you state the length of the period.*)

f. Have you ëver döne this ëxercise befóre?
Yès, | we've döne it ònce (twice, three times, etc.) beföre.
No, | we've nèver döne it beföre.

Learn these models by heart and repeat them as a dialogue. Then give a suitable response to each of the following commands or questions, basing your answer on one of the models above:

(*a*) Shut the window.   (*b*) Put your elbows on the table.
(*c*) Take them off again.   (*d*) Shut the window.
(*e*) Go to the door and then go back to your place.
(*f*) Open the book at page 16.   (*g*) Find the 8th line from the bottom.

(*h*) Have you read this page be-   (*i*) Turn to the next page.
fore?

(*j*) Read the first line.   (*k*) Start reading page 17.

(*l*) Have you finished page 17?   (*m*) Have you read the first line?

(*n*) (You're very slow) Haven't you finished page 17 yet?

(*o*) (You're very quick) Have you finished it already?

(*p*) Have you been to the dentist?   (*q*) How long have you had this
book?

(*r*) Since when have you been able to read English?

(*s*) Think of a number and write   (*t*) Here are five cards: choose
it down.   one.

(*u*) Have we finished this exercise? [20]

267.   (*a*) *Supply the missing verbs in a suitable tense:*

I did Exercise 266 yesterday, and performed certain actions. First
I — the window, then I — my elbows on the table and — them off
again. I — not — the window again, because it — shut already. But
I — to the door and then — back to my place. I — my book at page
16 and — the 8th line from the bottom. Then I — to the next page.
[10]

     (*b*) *In the following passage, change* every day *to* this morning (*i.e.
earlier in the day, in time which you consider past*) *and make the necessary changes in the verbs:*

Every day, I wake up at about seven. I lie in bed and read for five
minutes. Then I get up, wash, get dressed, and have breakfast. I leave
my house at eight o'clock, walk down the road and buy a newspaper.
Then I catch a 'bus. I pay my fare, and the conductor gives me a
ticket. The 'bus takes a very long time, but fortunately I am not late.
[15]

     (*c*) *Replace* today *by* yesterday, *and make other necessary changes:*

Today, I am not very well. Are you? And how is Thomas? And
how are the boys? It is rather cold outside, isn't it? This is an excel-
lent tea. (*Change* this *to* that). These are delicious cakes, aren't they?
(*Change* these . . .)

     (*d*) *Supply the missing verbs in a suitable tense:*

It — very wet yesterday, so I — indoors.

I — to you last week. — you — my letter?

— you — the latest news? Then listen.

— you — that shot (a moment ago)?

I — my leg last Thursday and — not — able to walk since.

Gandhi — born in 1869 and — in 1948.

— we — Exercise 264? Yes, we — it last week. [12]

Used to

268. **A father tells his children stories.** (*In the present*)
My father often told us stories when we were children. (*A past habit*)
Does your father tell you stories? (*In the present*)
He used* to tell us stories, but he doesn't now. (*Past habit: contrast with present*)

Use the Past Tense for repeated or habitual action in the past. Used to *emphasises the idea of habitual action in the past in contrast with present habit. Make up sequences, as in the examples above, beginning from the situations below. In the second line, supply a clause or phrase like* when we were children, fifty years ago, *etc.*

(*a*) Some mothers make their own children's clothes. My mother made our clothes herself . . .

(*b*) Some boys go to school by bus. I always went . . . Do you . . . ?

(*c*) Some people spend their holidays by the sea. We sometimes . . .

(*d*) Some people get up late. My parents usually . . . Do your parents . . . ?

(*e*) Some people keep money in a stocking. My grandmother . . .

(*f*) Some girls are shy. Jane . . . Is Ruth . . . ?

(*g*) One can wear a hat. Men always . . . Do they now?

(*h*) One can buy vegetables at the market. We generally . . . Does your wife . . . ?

(*i*) Choose your own ties. My husband . . . Does your husband . . . ?

(*j*) We find English very difficult. I . . . Do you . . . ?

269. **The Pre-present Continuous and Past Continuous**

**Every day, I study from 8 o'clock till 12. It is now 9 o'clock.
I am busy. I am studying. I have been studying for one hour.
What have I been doing?** (*Answer*)
**Suppose it is now 10 o'clock. I am tired. Why?
Because I have been working hard.
Yesterday, at 9 o'clock I was studying.
At 9.15, I was still studying.
What was I doing at 9.30?** (*Answer*)

---

* *In* use (*verb*) *and* used, *the* s *is soft; but in* used to, *the* s *becomes hard under the influence of the* t.

In present time, we use the Present Continuous Tense to emphasise the idea of action in progress, or uncompleted action, or the process rather than the act. In the Pre-present and the Past, we can use continuous tenses to make the same kind of emphasis. Repeat the sequence given at the beginning of the exercise, using rest, *then* read *then* play the piano, *and making other changes according to the sense. Then repeat the whole exercise, including the models, beginning:* Every day, you study . . . , *then* Henry studies . . . Ann studies . . . we study . . . the students study . . .

270. **It's 10 o'clock. It's raining. We can't go out.**
It's 11 o'clock. The rain has stopped. But the streets are wet.
Why? Because it has been raining.
Why didn't we go out earlier? Because it was raining.

Learn the models. Then complete the following, using the words in parentheses in a suitable tense and answering all the questions:

(*a*) Why is the wall so hot? (sun, shine on it)
(*b*) Why are you out of breath? (run up and down stairs)
(*c*) Is your father very ill? (Yes: work, too hard)
(*d*) Mary plays that piece very well. (No wonder; practise, six months)
(*e*) What was Mary doing three weeks ago?
(*f*) What was your father doing before he fell ill?
(*g*) You are learning English. Suppose you started learning two years ago. How long (learn English) till now?
(*h*) We are waiting for the doctor. We got here half an hour ago, so (we wait) for half an hour. What (we do) ten minutes ago?
(*i*) What are you doing? What (you do) this time yesterday?
(*j*) It is time to stop. What (you do) for the last ten minutes? [10]

The Pre-past

271. *Just as you use the* **Pre-present Tense** *when you look back on time preceding the present moment and are interested in some event* **before or until now,** *so you can use the* **Pre-past Tense** *when you look back from some moment in the past and are interested in an event* **before or until then.** *For example:*

(a) **I saw Michael* on Sunday for the first time this year.**
He had been ill: that is why I had not seen him for so long.

He had been (*contracted form:* he'd been) *and* I had not seen (*contracted form:* I hadn't seen) *are in the Pre-past Tense. Use that*

* *Michael:* pronounce [mìke-l].

140

*tense to make it clear that Michael's illness and my not seeing him occurred **before** the meeting on Sunday. If you said* he was ill, *that might mean that Michael was ill on Sunday. Now notice this example:*

(b) **Michael was still resting: he had not gone back to work yet.**

Yet *means* either *before or until now,* or *before or until then, and is therefore associated with the Pre-present or Pre-past Tense. Here it means until then, and is therefore associated with the Pre-past. In the following example:*

(c)   **Did you pass your examination? No, I failed.**
         Yoü fáiled?* But you had wòrked sö hárd!

*I am chiefly interested in the fact that you failed, **then,** and that your hard work had come **before then.** I could also say* you worked so hard *in that context: in that case my interest moves back to the time when you worked. In example (c) the Pre-past Tense gives a certain emphasis but the meaning would be basically the same if we used the Ordinary Past in that context.*

272. *Use the Pre-past Tense, therefore, when this tense is necessary for the kind of meaning in 271 (a) and (b), or when you wish to emphasise the idea of one past event being the **prelude** to another. It is not necessary to use the Pre-past Tense simply when events happen one after another. For example, we say:*

Caesar came, he saw, he conquered.

In that case, our point of interest moves forward with each new event.

273.   (a) **We looked for him all day. Then we gave up the search.**
             We gave up the search. We had looked for him all day.
             Had we looked everywhere? No, we hadn't looked every-
             where.
        (b) **We often went to the sea. Last year we went there again.**
             We went to the sea last year. We had often been there before.
             Had we always been to the sea? No, we hadn't always been to
             the sea.

Use one of these sequences with:

(*a*) We invited a lot of people. Then we gave a party.
(*b*) We ordered plenty of food. There was enough to eat.
(*c*) We usually rented a cottage. Last year we stayed in a hotel.
(*d*) My father was never ill till last year. Last year, he caught pneumonia (see 20).

* *Notice this way of asking a question.*

141

274. *Put the verbs in brackets in the Past or Pre-past Tense:*
(*a*) We (arrive) at the station ten minutes late. The train (leave already).
(*b*) We (arrive) without our luggage. We (leave) it all behind.
(*c*) I (meet) the new President last night. I (not, meet) him before.
(*d*) I (never see) him before, but I (rëcognise) him at once.
(*e*) John (know) him already: he (meet) him several years before*.
(*f*) We (find) our guide at the foot of the cliff. He (fall) from the top.
(*g*) He (lay) there for several hours, and (be) nearly frozen.
(*h*) When we (have) a good sleep, we (feel) much better.
(*i*) When they (reach) the end of their journey, they (travel) four thousand miles, and (climb) mountains that no one (ever, explore).
[20]

Pre-past Continuous

275. **At 10 o'clock it was raining. We could† not go out.**
By 11 o'clock the rain had stopped. But the streets were wet.
Why? Because it had been raining.
Why hadn't we gone out earlier? Because it had been raining.

Look at 270 and put the model for it into the Past or Pre-past Tense, as above. Then do the same with all of 270. Begin (g) with: 'This time last year'. *Begin (h) with:* 'This time yesterday'. *Begin (i) with:* 'This time yesterday' *and continue* 'the same time the day before'.

The Ordinary Future Tense

276. **Today is Monday. Tomorrow will be Tuesday. It will not be Wednesday. Will it be Thursday? No, it won't be.**

Form the **Ordinary Future Tense** *with* **will** *plus the* **infinitive.** *Contracted forms:* I'll, you'll, he'll, she'll, we'll, they'll. *Interrogative:* will I? *etc. Negative:* will I not *plus infinitive; contracted form* won't (17) I, *etc. Use* will *and* won't *for all persons, singular and plural. The Future can also be formed with* **shall** *plus the* **infinitive, in the first person singular and plural,** *e.g.* I shall see you on Thursday: we shall see each other then. *However,* will *is widely used for all persons and it is not a 'mistake' to use it with* I *and* we.

---

* *Say* ago *to mean* back from now; *but* before *to mean* back from then.
† Can *in past narrative becomes* could (8:1 *silent*). *Negative,* could not: *contracted form* couldn't. Can *has no infinitive or past participle.*

ACTIVITY SEEN FROM VARIOUS ASPECTS OF TIME

277.　　A. **Answer the telephone.**　B. **I'll answer the phone.**

Repeat, as a dialogue, with:

Write down this message. Take it to the captain. Tell him it's urgent. Don't make any mistake. Please come at once. Don't go. Carry this parcel for me. Find me a seat. Bring me a glass of water. Don't leave me. Be here again tomorrow. Write to me. Don't forget. Don't be angry. Do your best.

Future Continuous

278.　　　**What are you doing now? I am studying.**
　　　What will you be doing this time tomorrow?
　　　I will still be studying.

The Future has a continuous form, like the other tenses, with the same kind of emphasis. Fill the gaps below:

Every day, I study from 8 o'clock till 12.
It is now 9 o'clock. I am busy. I am studying.
I — — — for three more hours.
What — — — doing for the next three hours? (Answer.)
I am sorry, I can't go out before 12. Why? (Answer.)

Repeat with rest, read, play the piano, *as in 269.*

The Pre-future

279.　　　　**What is that book like?**
　　I will tell you next week. I will have finished it by then.

*Use the **Pre-future Tense**, formed by **will have** + **the past participle**, when you imagine yourself looking back from some moment in the future and when you are interested in some action performed **before or until then**. Use the sequence at the head of this exercise 5 times, beginning with the following questions:*

What do you think of the ëxhibìtion? (tomorrow)
How do you like Peter's new song? (on Thursday)
Whät is yöur imprëssion of the nëw mànager? (this evening)
How much space will you need for your àrticle? (tonight)
Whät do you advïse me to dò about this cäse? (think about it)

143

The Future in the Past

280. **Today I say, 'I will write: I promise.'**
Yesterday I promised I would* write.

Use the **Future in the Past** *(formed by* **would** + *the infinitive) when you imagine yourself looking forward from a point of view in the past. You will only need to use this tense† after the Past Tense of words like* say, tell someone, know, think, expect, promise. *Put the following into the Future in the Past, beginning with* I said, I told you, *or something similar:*

It will rain. It will be a busy day. It will be a long way. George will be late. He will bring us a bottle of wine. We will forgive him. I will tell you the answer.

We are going to leave, we are leaving, we leave, in the future.

281. (a) **We are going to finish this chapter** ⎫
     It is going to rain   ⎪
     (b) **The President is arriving**   ⎬ **tomorrow.**
     (c) **He arrives at half-past four**   ⎭

Use pattern (a) *to emphasise present indications of what the future will bring. 'Present indications' may be intentions or preparations* (We are going to finish this) *or they may be signs telling us what will happen* (It is going to rain—I feel it in my bones, I see the clouds, the barometer). *These indications point to some future event, i.e. we will finish, it will rain.*

Use pattern (b) *to express the idea that plans or arrangements for some future action have been made, so that the action has, in a sense, begun. Do not use it instead of* It is going to rain: *that is not a matter of plans or arrangements.*

Use pattern (c) *when a programme has been made and when you feel so certain an event will happen that you imagine it as completed.*

If you do not want to make any of these kinds of emphasis, use will *for the future, as in 276.*

282. *Study the following examples:*

(a) Tomorrow will be Tuesday. (*A simple statement of the future; or emphasis on the future event, not on any preparations for it.*)

(b) (*The telephone rings.*) I'll answer it. (*The question of intention or of preparations does not arise.*)

---

* Would *rhymes with* could.   † See note on 280.

(*c*) I have read your letter. I am going to study it carefully and answer it in a day or two. (*Here the question of a process of intention and preparation does arise, and I wish to emphasise it.*)

(*d*) I will (*or* shall) study your letter carefully. (*This is a statement of the future, without the emphasis made by example* (*c*).)

(*e*) I am going to sneeze. (*I feel it, I know the symptoms and I know what the result will be.*)

(*f*) We are discussing your case at our meeting next Friday. The ship is sailing at three. (*Arrangements have been made.*)

(*g*) We discuss your case next Friday. The ship sails at three. (*The discussion is on the agenda. The sailing is on the time-table. You can assume they will take place.*)

(*h*) We will (*or* shall) discuss it on Friday. The ship will sail at three. (*See note to example* (*d*).)

283. *The sentences below* (*not the sentences in parentheses*) *refer to future action. Use the* **words** *in parentheses to fill the gap. Choose the most suitable of the four ways of expressing the future given in 276 and 281 and give reasons for your choice.*

(*a*) (we, have) (Mother is busy in the kitchen.) What . . . for dinner?

(*b*) (come) (She has laid an extra place at the table.) Who . . . for lunch?

(*c*) (you, break) (You are sitting on a chair, leaning back.) Be careful . . . that chair.

(*d*) (sell) I . . . my car. Oh, what made you decide to do that?

(*e*) (collapse) (There is a fire.) Stand back. The roof . . .

(*f*) (carry) (I meet my old aunt unexpectedly. She is carrying a parcel.) Let me take that. I . . . it for you.

(*g*) (I, open) It's hot in here. . . . the window, if you like.

(*h*) (we, have) It is hot. I think . . . a thunderstorm.

(*i*) (be) How old are you? Twenty-four. I . . . twenty-five next month.

(*j*) (you, do). You're always engaged. What . . . this evening, for example?

(*k*) (leave, arrive) (What is your time-table for tomorrow?) I . . . here at eight and . . . in London at six in the evening.

(*l*) (have) In that case you . . . a tiring journey.

(*m*) (take place) Our meeting . . . on June 1st.

(*n*) (not, be: go) Mr. Williams . . . present. He (go) abroad.

(*o*) (see) Have you seen the doctor yet? Not yet. I . . . him this morning. I have an appointment at twelve.

It's time we went. I wish it was. I wish I were.

284. (a) You haven't gone yet. It's tïme you lèft.
         I'm not rich. I wïsh I wàs. I wïsh I wère.
     (b) I didn't go. I haven't gone yet. I wïsh I hàd (gone).
     (c) I haven't gone yet, but I will go. I wïsh you wòuld (go).

In (*a*) *the action* **has not taken place;** *we* **imagine** *it happening in the present but use the form of the Past Tense* (left, was). *When we think of the fulfilment as highly improbable, we can say* I were, he (she or it) were, *after if and* wish. *In* (*b*) *the action did not take place, or has not taken place: we imagine it happening in the past and use the form of the Pre-past* (had gone). *In* (*c*) *the action has not taken place, but we imagine it happening in the future and use the form of the Future in the Past. Use the form of the Past, Pre-past or Future in the Past to fill the following gaps:*

    (*a*) It's very late. It's time we — home.
    (*b*) George is still asleep. It's time he — up.
    (*c*) Waiter! We ordered coffee half an hour ago. It's time you — it.
    (*d*) I don't like this place. I wish I — far away from it.
    (*e*) I can never be President. Sometimes I wish I — .
    (*f*) George often behaves as if he — President.
    (*g*) I hear John's story was very funny. I wish I — it.
    (*h*) I'll ask him to tell it again. Oh, I wish you — him.
    (*i*) I saw John but forgot to ask him. Oh, I wish you — him.
    (*j*) Where is today's newspaper? I've burnt it. Oh, I wish you —.
I haven't read it yet. [10]

Sequence of Tenses

285. (a) I assure you. We have had a wonderful time and will come
          again.
     (b) I assured him we had had a wonderful time and would go
          again.

Choice of tenses depends on the speaker's point of view and the particular meaning he wishes to express. But, as in the examples above, we often find the following combinations of Tenses:

    (*a*) Present, Pre-present, Future.
    (*b*) Past, Pre-past, Future in the Past.

286. *In the following sentences, put the first verb into the Past Tense and make any other changes that are then necessary:*

    (*a*) I cannot understand him. Does he think we do not know how
to beháve (13)?
    (*b*) I promise I will not forget. I hope you will believe me.

TABLE 29

The English Tenses

Tense	Speaker's point of view	Direction of speaker's attention	Ordinary Tense	Continuous Tense
Present	Now	Now	I walk	I am walking
Pre-present	Now	Time before now	I have walked	I have been walking
Past	Then (*past*)	Then	I walked	I was walking
Pre-past	Then	Time before then	I had walked	I had been walking
Future	Then (*future*)	Then	I will walk	I will be walking
Pre-future	Then	Time before then	I will have walked	I will have been walking
Future in the Past	Then (*past*)	Time after then	I would walk	I would be walking

Notes. 1. *Past habit, contrasted with the present*—I used to walk.
   2. *Other ways of expressing the future:*

   (*a*) *Emphasis on present indications pointing to a future event, e.g.:*

   It is going to rain. You are going to break that chair.

   (*b*) *Emphasis on present (human) arrangements which are the beginning of an activity, e.g.:*

   George is coming to dinner tomorrow.

   (*c*) *Emphasis on a firm plan or time-table, e.g.:*

   His train arrives at eleven tomorrow morning.

(*c*) Night is falling. It has been a perfect day,
(*d*) but who can tell what tomorrow* will bring?
(*e*) We are sunburnt. The sun has been shining in our faces all day.
(*f*) Our leader is pleased. I think he really feels we have done our best.

* tomorrow *means* 'the day after today'. *In the past or future, say* 'the next day'.

147

(g) The wind is getting stronger. I am sure there will be a storm. Several boats have already returned to the harbour, and people are fastening heavy shutters against their windows.

(h) The damage is very serious. Twenty houses have been destroyed, and it will take days to clear the streets. [25]

TABLE 30

The Continuous Forms

I am studying every day for an examination. (*Emphasis on the idea that I am in the process of my studies.*)

I study every day from 8 to 12. (*No such emphasis; or emphasis on the whole operation, the regular series of acts.*)

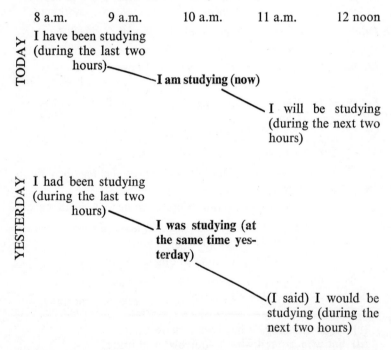

| 8 a.m. | 9 a.m. | 10 a.m. | 11 a.m. | 12 noon |

TODAY
I have been studying (during the last two hours)—
→ I am studying (now)
→ I will be studying (during the next two hours)

YESTERDAY
I had been studying (during the last two hours)—
→ I was studying (at the same time yesterday)
→ (I said) I would be studying (during the next two hours)

Note the use of during. *In saying* 'I have been studying' *we are interested in action in progress at any time* **during** *the two hours, or* **for** *the whole period.*

Miscellaneous Exercises in the Tenses and Irregular Verbs

287. *Put the verb in brackets into the most suitable tense. Where there is no verb given, think of a suitable one and put it in the appropriate tense.*

(*a*) In this chapter, we (deal) with irregular verbs. I — you (not, forget) them.

(*b*) 'Where (you, get) that bruise on your forehead (6, h *silent*)?' my wife — me this morning. I — up my hand and — a lump. Then I (remember). 'In the middle of the night', I — her. 'I — up and (think) I — a noise downstairs. You — fast asleep. I (creep) to the door, — it carefully, and —. Then I — the noise again. I (begin) to creep downstairs. Suddenly I (catch) my foot on a stick which someone (leave) on the stairs, and I —. I (wonder) you (not, hear) me. When I (pick myself up), I (find myself) at the bottom of the stairs. The front door — open and a man (stand) outside. He (shine) a light at me. Then I — he — a policeman. He — " — you all right, sir? (you hurt) yourself? I only (come) to tell you your door — open. I — you — to fasten it properly last night." I — him, — the door, — back to bed, and (sleep) soundly until you (wake) me up.' 'What (you do) with the stick?' my wife asked. 'Nothing', I —. 'I — not find it. It — probably still on the stairs and somebody (fall) over it again.'

(*c*) We (do) an exercise on the verbs. We (not, do) any more today: we (do) enough. (You get) them all right?

More Exercises in the Irregular Verbs

288.   **I don't want to hear your story. I've heard it already.**

For each of the 50 sentences below, make up another as in the model. Use the verb in italics and put it in a suitable tense. Use pronouns in the second sentence when you can.

1. I can't *bear* this muddle. (long enough already)
2. I wanted to *beat* John at tennis. (But he . . .)
3. When did term *begin*? (last month)
4. How did you *bend* this iron rod? (with my own hands)
5. That dog doesn't *bite*. (Don't you believe it! . . . just . . .)
6. Did the wind *blow* very hard last night? (Yes, roof off)
7. I *broke* the window. (How . . . ?)
8. Did you *bring* a message? (Yes)
9. Tell George not to *burn* it. (already)
10. Where did you *buy* that hat? (at a sale)
11. Did you *choose* it yourself? (No, Mary . . . for me)
12. How much did it *cost*? (a lot of money)

13. How did you *cut* your chin? (with a razor)
14. Why did the workmen *dig* this hole? (. . . to lay a drainpipe)
15. Can you *draw* a picture? (yesterday)
16. What do you *dream* about? (not, for a long time)
17. *Drink* up your coffee. (already)
18. Can you *drive* a car? (for years; and still do)
19. Will you have some more to *eat*? Thank you, but . . . a huge meal.
20. How long did the first men take to *fly* across the Atlantic? (in sixteen hours)
21. *Give* the conductor your ticket. (already)
22. How did you *grow* this lovely flower? (in a hot-house)
23. Why did you *hang* my picture there? (so that I can always see it)
24. Did George *hide* the other picture? (Yes, in the cellar)
25. Where did you *hold* the meeting. (in the public square)
26. When did you *know* the results? (late last night)
27. Where did the police *lay* the body? (at the side of the road)
28. Did the dead man's family *lead* the procession? (Yes)
29. Did anyone *lend* them a car? (Yes)
30. *Let* the cat out. (an hour ago)
31. Did you find anywhere to *lie* down? (Yes, on the deck)
32. Where did you *lose* your wallet? (in the street)
33. What did you *mean* when you said no? (exactly what I said)
34. Did you *put* the kettle on? (Yes, ten minutes ago)
35. *Ring* the door-bell. (Twice, but no one has come)
36. How did you get here so quickly? Did you *run*? (Yes, all the way)
37. How much did you *sell* your car for?
38. When did the travellers *set* out? (at day-break)
39. Did you *shake* the bottle? (yes, hard)
40. What did you *shoot* the lion with? (a rifle)
41. Where did the 'Titanic' *sink*? (in the Atlantic)
42. Don't *spend* all my money! (I'm sorry, already)
43. Don't *spoil* my picture! (Don't worry, not)
44. Where did you *spread* out your wet clothes? (in the boiler room)
45. Did the lion *spring* out at you? (Yes . . . as I was about to shoot)
46. Why did you *steal* my purse? (Nobody . . . still in your pocket)
47. It's dark in here. *Strike* a match. (two already, but they're wet)
48. What did you *tell* the driver? (to drive like mad)
49. Did Leander or Byron *swim* across the Hellespont? (Both)
50. I can't *wear* this shirt any longer. (for a week already)

Question Tags

289. I gäve you the mòney, dìdn't I? (I'm sure I did)
I dïdn't forgét, díd I? (I'm not sure now)
Thère, I dìdn't forgët, dìd I? (You have the money)
I was right after all, wasn't I?

*Add similar question tags to the following and read it as a dialogue
with either a falling intonation or a rising one (see 207) according to the
sense:*

A says:	*B says:*
(a) It is terrible weather.	(b) It was worse yesterday.
(c) It wasn't worse than this.	(d) You remember. It didn't stop once.
(e) But you weren't out in it.	(f) Yes, but I had a raincoat.
(g) It will be better tomorrow.	(h) It can't go on like this.
(i) John and George are brothers.	(j) They aren't alike.
(k) They went to the races on Saturday.	(l) They had never been before.
(m) They had often wanted to go.	(n) Well, they have been now.

Passages for Reading and Study

290. *Study the passage in 253. Make a list of all the verbs, and give
the subject and tense of each, thus:*

Subject + Verb	*Tense*
I had met	Pre-past
An African chief came	Ordinary Past

291. *Answer the following questions on 253, using a complete sentence
for each answer, as in the example.*

**Example: When did the African chief come to England? He came to
England when he was past sixty.**

(a) Where had the speaker met him? (b) How old was the chief?
(c) Had he ever left his own country before? (d) What kind of post
did he hold? (e) Where did he fly to? (f) Did he know his own
country well? (g) When did the speaker's friend go to call on him?
(h) What did the friend ask him first? (i) What were the exact words
of the friend's first question? ('How —— ?') (j) What did the friend
ask him next? (k) What were the exact words of the second question? (l) What did the visitor say in reply? (m) When had he had

151

a frightening experience? (*n*) Where had he gone? (*o*) What were the exact words used by the chief at the beginning of his story? (*p*) What did the chief do at Victoria Station? (*q*) Where did he stand? (*r*) What did he see come in? (*s*) When did the doors swing outward? (*t*) To what point did the train come nearer and nearer? (*u*) When did the men jump out? (*v*) Then what did they do? (*w*) How did they carry their umbrellas? (*x*) What were their faces like? (*y*) What did the chief think? (*z*) So what did he do?

292. *Write down the answers to the questions in 291. Then close your text-books, and form questions which will produce the answers you have written.*

MISCELLANEOUS TESTS

293. *Arrange the following words in rhyming pairs, as in 42:*

any, aren't, believe, bowl, build, can't, caught, city, climb, coast, comb, cost, crowd, daughter, drawn, dressed, dried, eye, field, fight, fonder, form, grey, guest, guide, her, home, key, killed, lose, loud, most, occur, owe, penny, pretty, quite, receive, refer, said, sealed, shoes, show, spread, they, their, thought, thunder, time, torn, tossed, tree, try, wander, warm, water, wear, were, whole, wonder. [60]

294. *Arrange the following in pairs so that each member of a pair has the same rhythm as the other. Example:* a hündred stèps, an ängry màn.

(*a*) Write the number of the exercise. (*b*) I'm surprised to hear it. (*c*) And what's the matter now? (*d*) Tomorrow will be Tuesday. (*e*) Thëre are some bröken rècords. (*f*) Put the letter in the envelope. (*g*) Don't think of it. (*h*) Hëre is a new machine. (*i*) A sharp pen-knife. (*j*) A healthy condition. (*k*) There are too many mistakes. (*l*) Margaret can't forget. (*m*) In a most reasonable way. (*n*) A steel cupboard. (*o*) Expensive tea. (*p*) He's arriving Monday. (*q*) Drive carefully. (*r*) Give me a glass of water. (*s*) A perfect day. (*t*) Across the Atlantic. (*u*) It's almost empty. (*v*) I wonder if it's raining. (*w*) A most important thing. (*x*) I never heard it. [12 pairs]

295. (*a*) *Spell the 3rd person singular of the Present (e.g.* breaks), *the Present Participle (e.g.* breaking), *the Ordinary Past (e.g.* broke) *and the Past Participle (e.g.* broken) *of:* arrive, begin, carry, choose, die, do, forget, go, lay, lie, lose, occupy, occur, offer, pay, quarrel, refer, rain, run, suffer, travel, try, wake, win, write. [25]

(*b*) *Say and spell the plural of:* city, country, detective story, duty, enemy, excuse, handkerchief, hero, history, holiday, house, lady, lens, loaf, match-box, mouse, mouth, path, potato, picture-gallery, radio, society, son-in-law, wife, woman. [25]

296. (a) *Fill each gap with one of the following:* boys, boy's, boys', buy, by, he's, his, its, it's, their, there, they're, to, too, two, your, you're, were, we're, where.

— are six — in this room. — — ten a moment ago. — are the others? We think they've gone home: — not sure. In any case, now — not here. I don't know these —: what are — names? This — name is Harold. And what is — age? — eighteen. — just had — eighteenth birthday. What are the other — ages? Tell them not to go. — — early — leave yet. Will you be going — the post-office on — way home? If you are, please — me some stamps. If — not, don't worry. Look at that dog: — limping. Poor thing, — broken — leg. [25]
Write out the above sentences, filling the gaps, but replacing all contracted forms by full forms (e.g. we've = we have).

(b) *Supply the missing letters:*

(i) You must pract— your English every day. D—ly pract— is nec—ary. Bel—ve me. Don't dec—ve yourself.

(ii) Mr. Foster is going to Buenos Aires on import— b—ness. He is starting on his j—ney im—diately. He has a wide know— and exp—nce of for—n countries.

(iii) Our next door n—bour is a g—v—ment off—al. He takes his work very s—iously.

(iv) Who knows w—ther the w—ther will be fine or not tomorrow? There is no s—n, either way. But people can find these things out s—entific—ly.

(v) Who was to blame? Whose f—lt was it? I must rec—ve all the blame: I was who—ly respons—le. [25]

297. *Revise the reading passages. Then answer the following questions on them, giving the answer first in a phrase, then in a complete sentence, as in the example:*

Example: (From 101) Whät is there in frönt of our hòuse? A smäll gàrden. There is a smäll gàrden in frönt of our höuse.
(From 101) (a) What do we grow in the back garden? (b) What can I see from my bedroom window? (From 102) (c) What kind of buildings are there in our town? (d) What kind of car does my brother drive? (From 103) (e) Who is Dr Freeman? (f) What is Mary like? (From 104) (g) What is a compass? (From 105) (h) What is a typewriter? (i) What is there at the back of a typewriter?

(*j*) What do we put behind the roller? (*k*) What does the hammer hit? (*From 142*) (*l*) Where is John spending his holiday? (*m*) Where is his room? (*n*) Where does he usually walk? (*From 143*) (*o*) What is Mr. Morris ordering? (*p*) What is he *not* ordering? (*From 212*) (*q*) What do we fasten the door with? (*r*) Which rock is a thousand feet high? (*From 213*) (*s*) What must one keep tea-leaves in? (*t*) What do some people put in their tea? (*From 252*) (*u*) Where does the taxi stop? (*v*) Where does one of the women lead us first? (*From 253*) (*w*) What kind of post did the chief hold? (*x*) Where did he walk to on his first day in London? (*y*) Who jumped out of the train? [25] *Write out the answers. Then, without looking at the book, make up sentences to produce those answers.*

298. *Fill each gap with a preposition or adverb, including a word like still, yet, etc. Note that a preposition, etc., may consist of more than one word. Put the verbs in brackets in a suitable tense. The whole exercise must make complete and connected sense.*

(*a*) The distance — X — Z is 40 miles. I (drive) that distance — one hour. The road — the two places (pass) — Y. Y is — the road, three-quarters of the way to Z. Y is therefore — this side of Z, and Z is — Y.

(*b*) It is now 9.55 a.m. I (leave) — Z — 5 minutes. I (not start) —, but my car is — the door, and I (wait) to start. I (start) — 10 o'clock. I (know) I (arrive) — Z — exactly 60 minutes. It is 9.59: it is time I (start) the engine. It is 10: now I am —.

(*c*) It is 10.10. I (drive). I (leave) X 10 minutes —, and now I (go) — X, and my car (travel) — Y. It (move) — the road at 50 miles an hour. It cannot go faster than that today because there are other cars —.

(*d*) There are — cars — the road: that is to say there are no pedestrians. People are not allowed to walk — the road: they must cross — the road by a foot-bridge. Cars go — the bridge. I (see) two people who (ride) bicycles — the track — me. I (drive) — them and soon they are — me.

(*e*) Now 10.30. I (drive) — 10, i.e. — 30 minutes. I (— complete) 20 miles. I (drive) — 30 minutes more, i.e. — 11. If I drive dangerously, I can arrive — five — 11.

(*f*) 10.50 (I arrive) — Z —? No, not —. 11.02. Now I (arrive). I (arrive) 2 minutes —. I (travel) 40 miles and (drive) — one hour.

(*g*) 11.30. I (leave) X — 10 and (pass) — Y on my way. — 10.30, I (drive), and five minutes later, I (— travel), — hundreds of other cars. I (leave) X 35 minutes —.

(*h*) 11.10. When I (be) — X, I (know) I (arrive) — one hour.

When I (be) at Y, I (travel) 30 miles, and (drive) three-quarters of an hour. — 9.55, I (not start) —, but I (wait) to start.

(*i*) When I (come) to Z, I (see) two people who (ride) bicycles. I soon (pass) them.

(*j*) I (drive) — Z alone, — a passenger. You (not come) — me. I wish you (come). [100]

299. *Say the following in a different but acceptable way, as in 145:*

(*a*) George is not up yet. (*b*) He woke up two hours ago. (*c*) Mary is still asleep. (*d*) You don't eat a great amount. (*e*) Some people overeat. (*f*) This boat is overcrowded. (*g*) That is what I firmly believe. (*h*) Take a deep breath. (*i*) He's a hard worker. (*j*) She makes her clothes herself. (*k*) I'm asking you what his name is. (*l*) The name of this material is nylon. (*m*) Get a chair for your guest. (*n*) You do not do enough practice. (*o*) This tea is undrinkable. (*p*) George always does what I tell him not to do. (*q*) A building made of wood. (*r*) The train that takes you to your business. (*s*) Take away these things. (*t*) Let's come away from this place. (*u*) I say to you, 'Is this the right road?' (*v*) Your room is above mine but not right over it. (*w*) I saw John when I was on my way home. (*x*) Please explain the meaning of this sentence to us. (*y*) It's late: we must stop now. [25]

300. *Arrange the words in the groups below so that each group makes complete sense. Put in suitable punctuation marks.*

(*a*) go, on, usually, the, Sundays, into, we, country.

(*b*) the, this, both, blue, old, my, Persian, room, rugs, are, in, uncle's.

(*c*) all, those, who, the, tomato, yesterday, dug, in, up, garden, plants.

(*d*) the, these, they, enough, wall, pictures, not, have, put, on, up, carefully.

(*e*) you, the, they, they, did, were, weren't, see, last, wonderful, night, fireworks.

(*f*) A, white, professor, was, was, were, talking, listening, walking, to, with, about, and, but, all, students, his, him, nobody, hair.

(*g*) we, him, Hudson, had, came, heard, never, anything, before, about, James, here.

(*h*) we, she, you, that, problem, have, not, asked, answered, worked, already, yet, out.

(*i*) she, we, it, us, had, worked, asked, if, properly, out.

(*j*) there, is, the, door, anybody, said, knocking, his, guide, on, there, with, the, stick.

155

NOTES AND ANSWERS

NOTES FOR TEACHERS AND ANSWERS
TO SOME OF THE EXERCISES

N.B. Other answers may be correct (see page 9). If in any doubt, adopt the answers given below.

Part One

Proficiency in English—perhaps more than in any major language—depends very much on a firm grasp of the vowel system, of the main principles of stress, rhythm and pitch, and of certain general rules of spelling. The chief purpose of Part One is to form correct habits of pronunciation and spelling which students can apply right through the course, and afterwards. Students who are the most eager to begin reading and expressing themselves freely are often those most likely to be held back by bad habits of pronunciation and spelling later.

Every student will want to know the meaning of the words and phrases he practises on, and you should give the meaning of words and phrases in Part One before you start exercising them. But remember that the best way to learn the meaning of words is to use them in a suitable context. Whenever, therefore, you can make natural use of the words and phrases given as examples, do so. For instance, the numbers are given as examples in Ex. 2 and are meant to be used immediately in English, in answering the questions in the rest of the exercise.

Table 1. This gives the English vowel sounds illustrated by words in frequent use. The first sound is the vowel sound in *see*; and so on. Teach sounds 1–12 as pure vowels, i.e. made with the tongue and lips in one fixed position. Make 1–4 with the front of the tongue raised; 5–9 with the back raised; 10–12 with the middle. These anatomical details are largely for the teacher's guidance. However, **keep Table 1 in your own and your pupils' minds right through the course.** Why not make a chart of it?

In practising the 'pure' vowels, start with 12, the vowel sound of the unstressed syllable in *better*. Make it with the tongue relaxed, in a neutral position; and make it short, i.e. take a comparatively short time over producing it.

Prolong No. 12 to get 11. Do not put any *r* sound in 11. There is no need for beginners to be aware of the possibility of an *r* sound in it at this stage.

Make 10 with a sudden opening of the mouth. Keep it short. Think of the sound and meaning of *sudden*.

Start with 12 again to get 2 and 8, which are also short and relaxed, and sound rather like 12. In fact, if your pupils confuse *live* with *leave*, tell them to pronounce *live* with 12 when speaking quickly and when it comes in the middle of a sentence. 2 is a small sound, as in *pin*.

Now go to No. 1. Feel the tongue move forwards and upwards and get more tense as you move from 2 to 1. Keep No. 1 long.

Open the mouth a little more widely as you move from 2 to 3, and again from 3 to 4. Make 3 short. Keep the jaw fixed for 4. Practise *pin, pen, hand, arm.*

Make 5 long, like an arm. Put no *r* sound in it.

6, short. Practise saying *hot* quickly, as if you have picked up something hot and drop it at once.

7, long, like the sound of a horn. No *r* sound, but a slightly smaller mouth opening than 6.

9, long, with a slightly smaller opening than 8.

Teach 13–19 as diphthongs, in which the tongue and lips move from the position required for one pure vowel to the position required for another. Make all the diphthongs long sounds, but give the first element more stress and length than the second. Let each diphthong glide towards the short relaxed sounds 12, 2 or 8, thus:

Number	Starting point	Gliding towards
13	Between 3 and 4	
14	Between 4 and 5	2
15	7	
16	Between 4 and 5	8
17	12	
18	2	12
19	3	

(Note: When 18 is unaccented, as in *Austrália*, make both elements short, with equal stress.)

Exercises 1–14 should be used, at first, only for practice in hearing and reproducing English sounds—not for identifying written symbols.

Exercise 1. Students should be able both to recognise and to reproduce these sounds correctly, to use both the numbers and the key words in identifying the vowel sounds in new words. Thus, *want*—vowel No. 6, as in *hot*. The most important thing is to hear and make the distinction between words likely to be confused.

2. Students should be very familiar with the words in heavy type in the instructions, e.g. **vowel.** Teach the numbers, up to 20, in English, and make the pupils answer in English. Then proceed thus: *one*—vowel number ten. Pronounce *four* with sound No. 7 in this exercise. Pronounce *seven* with one vowel, also *Table* and *Listen* (see note Ex. 11). Pronounce *eleven* as two syllables, *elèven* (2, 3), explaining that it is one word with two vowel sounds. Pronounce *vowel* as two syllables (16, 12). Give unaccented syllables a natural but clear pronunciation (see notes to Ex. 14). Be careful of *are* (5), *was* (6), *were* (11), *wòman* (8, 12), *wòmen* (2, 2), *child* (14), *chìldren* (2, 12), *key* (1), *word* (11), *one* (10), *not* (6) and *nought* (7). If in doubt about a pronunciation, work through this course thoroughly on your own; or consult a good pronouncing dictionary.

3. Be careful of *walk* (7), *work* (11), *law* (7), *wars* (7), *màny* (3, 2), *ònly* (17, 2). Count *ankle* (4) and *uncle* (10) as one vowel; and pronounce *more*

as 7 at this stage. Use this exercise as a test, and count the 'score' (maximum 100). Repeat the test and try to improve the result.

Table 1a. Four, more, door, etc. can be either 7 or 20.

$$\left.\begin{array}{l} \text{No. } 20 = 7 \\ 21 = 8 \\ 22 = 14 \\ 23 = 16 \end{array}\right\} \text{ gliding towards 12}$$

4. Pronounce *poor* as 21, though both 20 and 7 are common.

6. Make up exercises as necessary. However, do not spend too much time trying to achieve perfection. Go on with the course, let the students get accustomed to hearing the language, and drill difficult pairs as you come to them.

Table 2. In the column headed Sound, pronounce *b* like the second syllable of *rubber*; *p* like the first syllable of *perhaps; m* like the second syllable of *summer,* etc. Give *l* two pronunciations—one at the beginning of a word, as in *leave,* the other as in the second syllable of *table.* There is no letter of the alphabet for the middle consonant in *measure,* and the phonetic symbol [ʒ] is used for this sound in the Table. The sound [ʒ] does not usually occur at the beginning of English words; nor does the sound *ng.*

The 'soft' sounds are voiced, i.e. the vocal chords are open when these sounds are made. The 'hard' sounds are unvoiced or voiceless—the vocal chords are closed. The importance of this difference will be seen later. Note voiced *b* corresponds with unvoiced *p*; *v* with *f*; soft *th* with hard *th*; *d* with *t*; *z* with *s*; [ʒ] with *sh*; *g* with *k*. In the middle or at the end of a word, voiced consonants tend to be longer than unvoiced.

Consonants are made when the breath meets some obstruction as it passes through the vocal organs. With *b, p, m, w,* the obstruction is caused by the lips. English *p* at the beginning of a stressed syllable is accompanied by a sharp puff of breath, or aspiration. The sound *m* is nasal, i.e. the breath passes through the nose. Make *w* by putting the lips together, pushing them slightly forward and then drawing them quickly back: keep the tongue flat.

Pronounce *v* and *f* by placing the lower lip firmly against the upper teeth; *th,* by placing the tip of the tongue between the teeth.

Pronounce *d, t,* and *n* with the tip of the tongue against the upper teeth or teeth-ridge. Note that *t* is aspirated, like *p;* and *n* is nasal. To pronounce *l,* press the tip of the tongue against the teeth-ridge so that the middle of the mouth is closed and breath passes out at the side. To pronounce *r,* let the tip of the tongue lightly touch the teeth-ridge once, keeping the rest of the tongue low and contracted.

For *s* and *z,* raise the blade of the tongue to the teeth-ridge leaving a very narrow passage through which the air can pass: keep the teeth close together. For *sh,* raise the tongue as for *s,* but leave a wider passage at the front and a narrower one farther back. Push the lips forward and let the breath escape with a sharp hiss. [ʒ] is the voiced equivalent of *sh.*

For the consonant sound *y,* place the tongue as for vowel No. 2, then quickly pull it away and pronounce the vowel that follows.

Make *g*, *k* with the back of the tongue against the soft palate. Similarly with *ng*, letting the air pass through the nose. Note that *k* is aspirated, like *p* and *t*.

Practise *h* by forcing breath through the glottis. At the beginning of a word or syllable *h* must be pronounced (but see exceptions in Ex. 20). But do not pronounce it at the end of a word or syllable, e.g. *Oh!*

8. Pronounce *what, where, when,* etc. simply with the sound *w*. Do not worry about the voiceless *w* which is sometimes heard in these words. Pronounce *who, whose* with the sound *h*. Pronounce *pà/per, lès/son, to/mòr/row, nùm/ber, fin/ger* (see 9), *vil/lage, wèa/ther, sù/gar,* dividing the syllables as indicated by the oblique stroke. See note to 14.

9. Take care when a word ends in a consonant. Place the vocal organs in the position required for the consonant but release them softly without adding the sound of vowel No. 12. Say *rub this out* by placing the lips as for *b* and then placing the tongue as for *th*, without an intervening vowel sound. Pronounce *rùb/ber, stòp/per, sùm/mer, rùn/ner* as indicated, but with only one medial consonant sound. Pronounce *lò/ver, bà/ther* (13), *rì/der, wrì/ter, gà/rage, stù/dy, stù/dent.*

Note that *p* is less aspirated in the middle and end of a word than at the beginning. The same applies to *t* and *k*.

lived, stopped are words of one syllable; *en/ded* has two (see Table 26).

In *stronger, longer* (adjectives), *English, finger, single,* pronounce a *g* sound after the *ng* sound, and pronounce as *strong/ger,* etc. But do not do this with *singing, longing* (verbs) and *singer:* pronounce *sing/ing,* etc.

11. The accents and the numbers in brackets, e.g. *pèople* (1), will be explained later. They are given now for guidance during revision. *Table, people, little,* etc. have two syllables. Let the second consist simply of *b* (or *p,* or *t,* etc.) plus the 'dark' *l* sound (like the last sound of *pull*), without a vowel. Pronounce *table* as follows: sound *t*, vowel 13; then sound *b* followed by sound *l* as at the end of *pull*. If necessary, practise by saying *tày bull*. Similarly, pronounce *listen* as *l*, vowel 2; then *s*, followed by sound *n*, as in *sun.*

Table 3. In compounds (*j, ch, dr* and *tr*) two consonants come together so quickly that the first is not finished before the other begins. The two elements in *j* are *d* and [ʒ]; in *ch*, *t* and *sh;* in *dr*, *d* and *r;* and in *tr*, *t* and *r*. In the clusters (rest of the combinations in Table 3) pronounce two consonants in one articulation without a gap or vowel between, and be careful not to put a vowel *before* the clusters.

12. Do not allow a vowel between *John* and *George,* etc. Where there is no comma, as in *bright blue,* place the tongue etc. in position for *t*, keep it there for a second and then pronounce *blue* without completing the release of the *t*. Pronounce *jumped, packs, clothes* as one syllable. If *clothes* is too difficult at first, pronounce it like the verb *close,* which is what many people actually say in fluent conversation: but this applies only to the noun. Pronounce the verb, as in *He clothes us,* with the ending soft *th* + *z*.

13. Note the consonant sound *y* at the beginning of the pronunciation of the letter *u*, and of the words *useful, united, university,* etc. Note also that *y*

often precedes vowel No. 9 as in the words in 13 (b). This is indicated thus: *view* (y + 9). Do not insist on the *y* sound after *d* or *t* if the student has already learnt a different acceptable pronunciation.

14. A mark like \, ·· or / (see 28–39), indicates that the syllable containing the vowel sound whose symbol is thus marked is accented. Be careful to accent the right syllable and always pronounce the vowel in the accented syllable fully and accurately. When teaching a new word or speaking deliberately, as in dictation, pronounce the unaccented syllables clearly, too. However, in many unaccented syllables, the vowel becomes simply No. 12 in fluent speech, e.g. in *cònsonant, photògrapher*. In others, it becomes No. 2, e.g. in *pràctise, explàin, knòwledge*. Long vowels and diphthongs in unaccented syllables tend to keep their full value, e.g. *rècord* (3, 7), *tomòrrow* (8, 6, 17), though even in such cases No. 12 in the unaccented syllables may be acceptable, as in *tomörrow mòrning*. Pronounce *thirteen, fourteen*, etc. with the stress on both syllables to avoid confusion with *thirty, forty*, etc. However, in the series, 13, 14, 15, etc. the syllable *-teen* generally loses its stress though it keeps the quality of its vowel sound (No. 1). This loss of stress commonly occurs on the repetition of a syllable or word.

In this exercise, words of more than one syllable are divided *in print* according to their etymology. This division is traditionally observed on paper when it is necessary to put part of a word on one line and part on another. Students should be advised not to try dividing words in writing until they are sufficiently advanced to understand the principles involved. Modern pronunciation does not always coincide with etymology in this respect. Thus, the first sound of the accented syllable in *explanation* is *n*. This is indicated by the sign ◡. Thus the second syllable of *English* begins with the sound *g*.

Note: *rècord, òbject* (nouns); *recòrd, objèct* (verbs).

Do Ex. 14 first deliberately, then more fluently. The key is given for the teacher's guidance only. The pronunciation in brackets indicates more fluent speech:

    (*a*) 2 + 2; 10 + 12; 4 + 2; 2 + n; 3 + 12 + 14.

    (*b*) 9 + 2 + 8; 9 + 2; 8 + 13 (12 + 13); 8 + 6 + 17 (12 + 6 + 17); 3 + 12 + 13 (3 + 12 + 2).

    (*c*) 7 + 2; 5 + 12 + 9; 1 + 2 (eve = 1 syllable); 10 + 13 (10 + 2); 9 + 13 (9 + 2).

    (*d*) 3 + 13 (3 + 2) (pronounce *Wednes-* as *wenz*); 11 + 13 (11 + 2); 14 + 13 (14 + 2); 4 + 12 + 13 (4 + 12 + 2); 10 + 13 (10 + 2).

    (*e*) 11 + 1; 11 + 2; 7 + 1; 7 + 2; 2 + 1; 2 + 2.

    (*f*) 17 + 12 + 5 (or 4); 12 + 6 + 12 + 12; 17 + 12 + 4 + 2; 4 + 12 + 13 + 12.

    (*g*) 3 + 13 (2 + 13); 3 + 4 + 13 + 12 (3 + 12 + 13 + 12); 17 + 16 (12 + 16); 6 + 10 + 2 + 13 + 12 (12 + 10 + 2 + 13 + 12).

    (*h*) 17; 6 + 3 (6 + 2); 4 + 2 + 12; 4 + 2 + 3 + 12 + 2 (in fluent speech, the 4th syllable may be omitted).

    (*i*) 10 + 12 + 12 + *l* (in fluent speech, the 2nd vowel sound may be omitted); 5 + 19; 13 + 2 + 17; 3 + 2 + 2 + 12.

(*j*) $3 + 7$; $3 + 7 (2 + 7)$; $6 + 3 (6 + 2)$; $6 + 3 (12 + 3)$; $2 + 7 + 12$; $3 + 3 + 3 + 2 (3 + 12 + 12 + 2)$.

The Alphabet. Students should be able to spell in English, and to put lists in alphabetical order.

Table 5. Many English words follow this scheme, and native speakers of English frequently use it when reading new words or when spelling phonetically. In this book, use it as a key to pronunciation, unless a number in brackets after the word indicates something different. (It may be necessary to explain that English spelling has remained largely unchanged for centuries, while the pronunciation, of vowels particularly, has changed considerably.)

Pronounce -*ook* as 8, otherwise -*oo* as 9, though see exceptions in 18. Note *pin* (2), *pine* (14); *not* (6), *note* (17); *hat* (4), *hate* (13); *get* (3), *scene* (1); *car* (5), *care* (19); *her* (11), *here* (18); *fir* (11), *fire* (22); *pay* (13), *pain* (13); *boy* (15), *boil* (15). This gives a useful guide to the pronunciation of a good many monosyllables.

18. Note that *after, half, branch, can't, dance,* etc. are also pronounced with No. 4. Do not insist on 5 if the student has already been taught 4. Words like *translate* may be pronounced $4 + 13$ or $5 + 13$ by the same speaker. Pronounce *wear* and *where* exactly the same (see note to 8). *Tear* (18) is a drop of liquid coming from the eye; *tear* (19) is an action. *Room* can be 8 or 9. *Bow* has different meanings according to its pronunciation.

19. *Talking:* the inflexion (e.g. -*ing*) at the end of a word is unaccented. *Ènglish* (2), *stùdent* (y + 9), *stùdy* (10): in this book one number in brackets immediately after a word indicates the pronunciation of the vowel in the stressed syllable. If the word has only one syllable, that one is, of course, the stressed one. More than one number, e.g. Good-bye ($8 + 14$), indicates the pronunciation of the separate vowels in the order in which they occur.

20. Use Table 2 and Ex. 20 as guides to the pronunciation of consonants, unless something different is indicated. Pronounce *pneumonia* (new + *mòan* + unstressed 18). Pronounce *psychology* (*sigh-còllogy*).

Notes of the pronunciation of *r*. Pronounce *r* whenever it begins a word or syllable, or when it comes before a suffix or word beginning with a vowel. It is not necessary (though it is usual in some important forms of English) to pronounce it in *car, care, near, her, here, fir, fire, for, more,* etc. Pronounce it in *nearest, here is, there are, far away, take care of it.*

The *s* of the plural of nouns and the 3rd person singular, Present Tense, of verbs, is pronounced *z* after a vowel or voiced consonant, and pronounced *s* after a voiceless consonant. Otherwise, final *s* is sometimes pronounced soft (as in *is, has, please*), sometimes hard (as in *house, us*).

Do not pronounce *w* at the end of a word, as in *law, saw, throw away.*

21. Read this to your students and explain what it means before they read it themselves. Do the same with 22.

22. The stress and intonation marks (see 28–39) are at first for the teacher's guidance. The student should follow them when he revises this exercise after finishing all of Part One.

23. Use dictation as an exercise in listening carefully, in reproducing something that makes sense, and in spelling.

25. Stress. Certain words in a sentence are pronounced with stress. They are the words which the speaker feels should be emphasised in the circumstances in which he is speaking. While syllable-stress is more or less fixed, word-stress within a sentence can vary according to where the speaker wants to put the emphasis. Some little words are so often unstressed that they develop a weak pronunciation, like the weakened syllables within a word. The pronunciation of these weak forms is indicated in the third column of Ex. 25 and by italics in the examples. Note that the strong form is used in deliberate speech, or in hesitation, or when the word receives emphasis, or stands in an exposed position, e.g. at the end of the sentence. However, the weak forms for *us* and *them* can be used even at the end of a sentence, when those words are unstressed. Use *a* before a consonant sound, including the first sound in words like *university.* Use *an* before a vowel sound, including words beginning with a silent *h.* Do not try to abbreviate *is* after a hissing sound (*s, z, sh, ch*). Weak *is* becomes *z* after a vowel or voiced consonant, *s* after a voiceless consonant. The vowel in weak *the* is 12 before a consonant sound, 2 before a vowel. Weak *to* has 12 before a consonant, 8 before a vowel. *For,* even when weak, has an *r* sound before a vowel. Weak *it is* is written *it's*—not to be confused with *its* (see 112 a).

26. Let the pupils make up as many examples as they can in a given time, so long as the examples make sense. However, make sure that in using the articles (*a, the*) they follow a common pattern of usage: see, for example, 54 and 78.

27. Rhythm makes language more enjoyable to speak and more attractive to listen to. It compels attention, helps us to remember, and is an important factor in many fixed expressions and common patterns of speech. In English it depends on a regular beat of stressed syllables, and on an equal interval of time between each stress. Notice how the spacing of the stresses, combined with the use of long or short vowels, or with an easy or difficult movement of the tongue from one position to another, affects the tempo of the line. For example, line *j* begins with six rapid notes, followed by a long one. See note on 29.

28–39. Pitch and Intonation are important factors in English. Intonation is the tune produced by changes of pitch as the voice moves during, away from, or towards a stressed syllable, or from one stress to another. It expresses a good deal of meaning. There are many varieties and subtleties of intonation which are not indicated in this book. The learner can best acquire them by hearing and imitating people who speak English naturally and well, or by studying them for himself later.

The large sign ◥ indicates a fall in pitch during the pronunciation of a stressed syllable; ◢ rise in pitch. ◦ indicates that an accented syllable is followed by an unaccented syllable at a lower pitch; ◢ rise in pitch, starting on a stressed syllable and still continuing on the following un-stressed syllable.

Difference in 'meaning' between falling and rising intonation. Assume that the falling tone is (a) normal, or (b) an indication of finality; while the rising tone indicates that there is something more to be said, either because there is more to follow, or because the speaker is expressing doubt or sur-prise or wants more information, or perhaps because he wants to let his audience feel that he has not said the last word. Note that a question can have either intonation. *Whät is thìs?* suggests *Thät is äll I wänt to knòw.* But *Is this trúe?* suggests *I wänt to knòw mòre: I am not certain whether the answer is 'Yes' or 'No'.* Normally, use a falling intonation with questions, unless they require the answer 'Yes' or 'No'.

29. Note that while *water, garden,* etc. have a similar pattern of stress and pitch, the length of the syllables varies. In *garden,* the first vowel is long; in *city* it is short. Length is also affected by the nature and combination of consonant sounds. See notes on Table 1 and 2 regarding length of sounds.

30. When more than one stress occurs in a sentence, start the first stress at a relatively high pitch, drop down on the next stress, and so on until the 'nucleus' is reached, when the ⟍ pattern or the ⟋ pattern occurs. Pro-nounce unstressed words at the beginning of a sentence on a low pitch before jumping up to the first stress point in the intonation pattern. After ⟍ pronounce any remaining syllables on the same low note: after ⟋ , on the same high note, rising at the end.

Strong emphasis or emotion can be expressed by special stress, accom-panied by a sharp fall or rise in pitch, e.g.

Stop!   What?   Go away

Simplified Method of Marking Stress and Intonation

The following system is used in this book whenever guidance has been thought to be necessary or helpful.

(i) Stressed syllables are marked with \, /, or ¨ over the vowel. Although the stressed syllable usually begins with a consonant, the vowel has been chosen to bear the stress-mark partly because that method raises no problem in printing, as it does not require special type. It also has the ad-vantage of drawing attention to the stressed vowel which the student must be particularly careful to pronounce correctly: see note on 14.

(ii) The sign \ indicates falling intonation, starting on a stressed syllable; the sign / indicates rising intonation on a stressed syllable. The sign ⌣ indi-cates an intonation beginning with a fall and ending with a rise: see 39. The rise or fall is the nucleus of the intonation pattern. Sometimes a rise occurs after the nucleus as a sign that we wish to modify what has gone before.

The sign ¨ indicates a stressed syllable occurring before or after the nucleus. When stresses come *before* the nucleus, begin the first on a relatively high pitch, then drop down a little on each stress, finally falling or rising on the nucleus. *After* the nucleus, pronounce each stress on the same pitch, low or high, as was reached by the fall or rise.

(iii) When a word has more than one stress, e.g. *ünderstànd, äfternòon*, follow the same intonation pattern as in (ii) and give prominence to the final stress. However, in many compound words, e.g. *pòst-öffice*, the first element is given prominence.

(iv) The sign | indicates the end of an intonation pattern before the end of a sentence. After | begin the pattern again, as in (ii).

N.B. Students are expected to read and repeat the examples in this book with the stress and intonation indicated; but they are not expected to assume that these indications are the only possible ones, except with regard to *syllable stress within a word*. With that exception, therefore, students need not *learn* how the indications are given.

31. Follow the instructions in the notes of Ex. 30, including the note on special stress.

32. Say the additions on the same final low pitch, with an extra little drop at the end.

34. Note the loss of stress on repetition of a syllable or word in examples c, j and k.

37. Say the additions on the same final high pitch, with an extra rise at the end.

38. Use a rising tone also at a break in the middle of a long sentence when the descent in intonation might otherwise be too long, e.g.

> *A bïrd in the hánd | is worth twö in the bùsh.*

39. In expressions which are meant to be polite, a falling tone can sound final, abrupt and dictatorial. A rising tone after the initial fall softens this effect.

42. (a) Examples: *are, car; bed, head; break, make;* etc.

(d) to (m): give as *unseen* dictation. Test ability to distinguish sounds and to give an appropriate spelling for the sound dictated. Vary the order or insert different words, in case students have prepared the test beforehand. But be sure you dictate the sounds you intend, and keep a note of the order in which you dictate them.

Part Two

Exercises 43–52. A mass-word refers to a thing in general, or a sample of it, not divided into separate units; e.g. a solid substance, or liquid, activity (such as *work*, *play*), thought or feeling. Abstractions such as *beauty* or *truth* come into this category, so long as we imagine them as something undivided and not as separate units.

43. *earth*, i.e. the substance in general, not the planet. Similarly *bone*, *hair* in general; *glass*, the substance, not the drinking vessel, etc. Do not

merely translate these words. Let your pupils see or imagine examples of the things the words refer to, so that a direct association is made between the thing and the English word. The words can be learnt through thoughtful use in the exercises that follow, or better still, in a natural context.

44. From now on, a model is given in heavy type, at the head of many of the exercises. The model should be properly understood, and then practised orally with correct pronunciation and intonation (see Part One). It should be learnt, and then imitated. In 44-47 inclusive, the mass-word refers to the thing in general. *Answer* 44 with words from 43, e.g. *Meat is flesh. Mud is earth. Music is sound. Science is knowledge. Leather is skin.*

47. A few verbs are introduced here simply to give additional practice with nouns.

In 48-51 inclusive, the mass-word refers to a sample of the thing, not the thing in general.

48. Distinguish between *this* (near the speaker) and *that* (away from the speaker). *It* refers to the thing mentioned.

49. Note *fresh air* (*water, meat, bread*); *stale bread; strong* or *weak tea* (*coffee*).

52. *Some* gives the idea of a small quantity of the mass (see 127, where *some* will be given special treatment). Compare *Give me some water* with *This is water* (48): in 48 emphasis is on the thing itself, the class of thing, without reference to quantity.

Exercises 53-64. These deal with words referring to things seen or imagined as separate whole units, many having definite shape (see 56) or being measurable.

53. Again do not merely translate, but make a direct association between thing and English word whenever you can. A drawing or picture will often help to establish this association.

Exercises 54-59. In these exercises, *a line*, etc. refers to one example of that class of thing, with emphasis on the *class*. In Exercises 60-64, *a pencil*, etc. refers to one example, with emphasis on quantity as well as class. Notice what happens when these ideas are expressed in the plural, Ex. 70, 71 and 72. Thus the plural of *a line* (54) is *lines*, but the plural of *a stamp* (64) is *some stamps* (72). Notice the use of *one* instead of *a* in 64 to emphasise the idea of 'one, not two or more', or of 'one as distinct from another'.

55. *Answer:* An ant is an insect, etc.

56. A *ball* (*watch, clock*, etc.) is also round. The students should have a clear idea of the shape of objects and the shape indicated by certain adjectives.

59. Prepositions (*to, at, in*, etc.) will receive special treatment later. Answer to (i): *We work at a table or desk* (or *at a shop or office*).

60. Dialogue between A and B. Note the shift of emphasis in *Thère is a pëncil* (emphasis on the *place indicated*), *Mìnd! There's a neèdle* (emphasis on the *thing mentioned*), *There's a pëncil in your pòcket* (emphasis on the existence of the thing mentioned in the place mentioned, and disappearance of emphasis on the place *indicated*). Note also: *There is some water* (*some sugar, milk, ink, paper*).

64. Dialogue between A and B.

65, 66. The general principle is that the noun takes no article when it refers to the thing in general, and takes an article when it refers to an isolated, whole example of the thing. However, this principle cannot be applied equally to all nouns. Thus, *a paper, a glass, an iron,* refer to certain classes of objects only; and some words, e.g. *money, music, furniture, information, advice, progress* are not normally used with the *in*definite article at all. These details can best be learnt by observation of actual usage and by experience of the language through reading and conversation. In Exercises 65 and 66, the teacher should work through the examples himself with beginners before letting them attempt the exercises on their own. *Answers:* 65. (*a*) light, a light; (*b*) a fire, fire; (*c*) time, a time (or *time*), a time (or *time*); (*d*) space, a space; (*e*) pleasure, pain, a pain; (*f*) an (interesting) life, life; (*g*) fuel, a fuel (or *fuel*), a fuel (or *fuel*), a food (or *food*); (*h*) a pleasure.

66. (*a*) piece of paper, paper, some paper, a paper; (*b*) glass, piece of glass, a glass; (*c*) piece of iron, an iron; (*d*) cloth, piece of cloth, a cloth; (*e*) some money, Money; (*f*) a game, job, work, play; (*g*) some information, piece of information; (*h*) some advice, piece of advice; (*i*) some furniture (or *furniture* alone), piece of furniture; (*j*) progress.

70. *Birds fly,* i.e. things of that class, in general: emphasis on class. Possible answer to (*k*): *Men wear suits and shirts. Women wear dresses.*

71. *Lines.* Here we are not referring to things of that class *in general,* but to more than one example of a thing of that class, with emphasis on class. Be careful to distinguish in pronunciation between *this* and *these* and in meaning between *these* (near the speaker) and *those* (away from the speaker). *They:* the things mentioned.

72. *Some stamps:* i.e. a small quantity of things of that class. For pronunciation of *some,* see Ex. 25 and notes.

73. In this exercise, *the* serves as a signal that we are specifying one particular example of a class of thing, as distinct from another, and that we assume our audience knows which example we mean. Note the stress pattern.

74. Here, *the* serves as a signal that we are specifying a thing of one class as distinct from something of another class. Note the stress pattern.

75. Here, *the* serves as a signal that we are specifying something already introduced. We know from the context what key is meant.

77. Here, *the* serves as a signal that we are referring to an object which is normally considered the unique example of its class. There can be other suns, but this is the one we usually mean.

78. Here, *the* serves as a signal that we are referring to some marked and known part of the map of our experience. There can be other ceilings, but we have only one in mind when we say *the ceiling.*

80, 81. 80 (*a*) is like 73, but in the plural; 80 (*b*) like 74 plural; 80 (*c*) like 75; 80 (*d*) like 76; 81 like 78. A plural example of 77 would be *the stars.*

82. In *to school, by bus,* etc. we are not primarily concerned with a specific school or bus, but with activity communally associated with those things.

169

Expressions like *go to school* are accepted conventions: you are not free to invent them for yourself.

83. *The water:* here we are specially concerned with a particular sample of water—this sample as distinct from the rest.

85. The subject of the sentence is *water* (singular) and the verb must therefore be *is* (see 162).

86. The sign **/** indicates contrast. *Pretty* and *beautiful* can both be contrasted with *ugly*.

90, 91. Note the stress and pitch: *stŏne wàll, bĕdroom wìndow*. Do not use *golden* or *silken* except in recognised metaphorical or poetic expressions.

Answers to 91: a drawing-room carpet; my office desk; your garden gate; a village doctor; the station clock; our school hall; the city walls; a university examination; a government official; a mountain road; a winter evening; an October morning.

92. Note the stress and pitch: *spàce shĭp, tòoth-brush*, etc. However, though the second element is on a lower pitch than the first, it usually retains some stress and the full vowel value of the separate word. In Ex. 92 pronounce the second element, in every case, with the full vowel value of the separate word, e.g. *flower* (23) *shop* (6). Point out that in some old compounds, e.g. *penknife*, a meaning is produced which is now different from that of both elements separately. The use of hyphens is very difficult to describe systematically. Generally speaking, a new combination, e.g. *space ship*, has no hyphen; the hyphen tends to be used as the combination becomes more familiar; then a new compound is formed, e.g. *penknife*. In this matter, the student can only observe usage and consult a good dictionary. Note that *oil, powder, paste* are mass-words, therefore say *it's hair-oil, it's face-powder, it's tooth-paste*. Note: *note-book, tooth-brush*.

93. *Answers:* sunny weather, sun-glasses; rainy weather, rain-coat; a windy day, wind instrument; a soap factory, soapy water; sandy soil, stony ground; beautiful girls, beauty competition; music lessons, musical; danger sign, dangerous corner; science teachers, scientific; poisonous, poison bottle.

94. *Answers:* This is soft yellow sand; some fresh white bread; the deep blue sea; that warm water in the basin; my black sun-glasses; etc.

95. *Answers:* (*a*) etc. This story is interesting. (*b*) This story is about war. (*d*) This cupboard is for china. (*f*) This juice is from grapes. (*l*) This bottle is for beer. (*j*) This official is in the government.

96. Use *healthy* attributively to refer to a permanent condition. Except in traditional, fixed expressions (e.g. *It's an ill wind that blows nobody any good*—meaning a very bad wind) do not use *ill* attributively; and it is advisable to avoid using *dear* attributively when referring to price.

97. Avoid *a ripe, some ripe*, etc. without a following noun. Note the special use of *the living*, etc. referring to people of that class in general, as in 70. Do not use this construction in any other sense.

98. You can invent compounds on this model, e.g. *a roomful, a houseful, a tankful*, etc.

100 (*d*). See *English as a Foreign Language* for *London University, the London Library*. Note which of these forms happens to be used when you come across them.

103. Note *the Freemans*, following the scheme in 67.

106. Answer with words or constructions occurring in 44 onwards. Beware of alternative possibilities. *A corn* can be right; it depends what you have in mind. If you mean '*corn*' (i.e. grain) in general, then *a corn* is wrong. *A fruit* is right, if you mean a kind of fruit. We can say *rain*, in general; or *the rain*, i.e. the rain that is now falling, or *the rain* as distinct from *the wind*. *Stone*, substance; *a stone*, object. *The world* (the one we all know) or *a world*. An answer is 'right' if it expresses exactly what the speaker has in mind.

108. Tell the students not to use *the* unless they are referring to a specified thing. *Answers:* (*a*) water, a bath, matches, a box, beer, barrels. (*b*) Fire, ash. The smoke, fire. (*c*) the ash, a cigarette, an ash-tray. (*d*) Sheets, cotton, blankets, wool. (*e*) A car, a machine, A carpet, an article, furniture. (*f*) A loaf, bread, some milk, some biscuits. (*g*) the post-office, some stamps. (*h*) a new hat, a good one. (*i*) hats, the brown one. (*j*) a hot day, the food, ice-box. (*k*) school, bus, home, foot. (*l*) school, science, mathematics. (*m*) Students, law, medicine, (a, the, or no article) university. (*n*) some ink, some ink, the bottle. (*o*) a letter, the date, the top, the paper. (*p*) wonderful weather, a cloud, the sky. (*q*) room, the light, the switch. (*r*) the capital, the Philippine Islands. (*s*) The river Ganges, the Himalayas, the Bay of Bengal. (*t*) heat, light, sound. (*u*) a good knowledge, English, progress. [70]

109. *Answers:* Cities are big towns; villages are small places. On summer evenings, we have meals in the open air. Book-shelves are long boards or sheets of metal. Knives are instruments with sharp blades. Put these matches and these leaves in those boxes. Write answers to the following questions. In the pictures, we see men, women and children. Mothers-in-law are the mothers of husbands or wives. There are some ladies and gentlemen outside. There are some sheep in the fields and (some) wolves in the forest.

113 (*c*).   Note the use of *some* in this kind of affirmative sentence, and *any* in this kind of interrogative and negative sentence. But do not insist that *some* must always be used in the affirmative, and *any* always in the negative and interrogative. See 127.

116. *James's* has two syllables (*James-iz*). Pronounce *Church's* like *churches*. Avoid *s's* after non-English names or long names. Say, for example, *Sóphocles' pläys* or *the pläys of Sòphocles*.

117 (*b*). *Answers:* It's Napoleon's hat, Shakespeare's theatre, the President's birthday, Dante's birthplace, a play about Caesar's death.

117 (*c*). i.e. my brother's home, the baker's shop, etc.

121. All the answers can follow the pattern of stress and intonation in *ròad-sïde*, but *sëa-sìde* and *wëek-ènd* are very common.

122. Use 116, 120 and 121 as guides in doing this exercise.

123 (*c*). 16, 18, is 23, is 41, is 16.

128. *Answers:* All earth is solid, but not all earth is hard. All the earth in this garden is soft, etc.

Table 9 and 131. In common usages, as in 131 (*b*), we tend to avoid using *little* and *few* without a modifying adverb.

132. Note: When there are only 5 gallons in it (rising intonation), the tank is half empty (fall). The tank is half empty (rise), when there are only 5 gallons in it (fall).

134. *Much or little: How much?* Note that in the question we normally use the word which indicates the higher degree. Similarly, *how old*, etc.

135. Note that in this kind of situation we avoid using *much, many, far, long*, by themselves in affirmative sentence. These words can, however, be used in affirmative sentences of greater length or in more formal style.

136. *Answers:* a piece of meat weighing 3 kilos. The piece is $2\frac{1}{2}$ kilos. It is not heavy enough, etc.

143. Notice the stress patterns in *Òxford Ròad*, but *Nòrth Street*.

144. *Answers:* (*a*)What, someone (somebody), the; (*b*)Who, It's. (*c*)are some; is also a. (*d*) Which, more, the. (*e*) all, are important, some, this, very (or most) important, it, an (or any). (*f*) no, the (or your), Whose. (*g*) Charles's, who. (*h*) He, of mine, best (or any other suitable adjective), He, one of the, this (or that). Which. (*i*) The, the, what, next (or second, or last, etc.). (*j*) his, my letters, any. (*k*) something, else. (*l*) anything, some, ice.

145. *Answers:* 1. What letter is that? 2. Who is that? 3. Whose is this towel? 4. That towel is hers. 5. Your father's name. 6. Your parents' address. 7. An elephant's trunk. 8. The road-side. 9. An evening's work. 10. I have no idea. 11. Everyone (or everybody) is happy. 12. Anyone (or anybody) can tell you. 13. Ask someone (somebody) else. 14. There is very little time. 15. There are very few plates. 16. But there is plenty (a good deal) of bread. 17. The basket is empty. 18. The box is nearly (almost) full. 19. This is a different box. 20. But is it the same size? 21. Answer the next question. 22. It is cooler today. 23. Tin is lighter than lead. 24. (3 + 4) is twice as much as (2 + 3). 25. This is as long as that. 26. I am as old as you. 27. What size is this room? 28. Give me another one. 29. Where are the others? 30. Both my sisters are married. 31. My brothers-in-law are doctors. 32. A doctor's life is a busy one. 33. His day is too short. 34. This chair is not high enough. 35. It is not so low as the next one. 36. Harold is younger than Peter. 37. Peter is Harold's elder brother. 38. Your work is better than mine. 39. Mine is better than his (His is not so good as mine). 40. Yours is the tidiest. 41. I can't understand all of this. 42. The room is half empty. 43. Here is another (one more) example. 44. This is private property. 45. This belongs to me, to nobody else. 46. I don't like such weak tea. 47. I don't like coffee as strong as this. 48. Mr Porter is a music teacher. 49. Ralph is a student of his. 50. I can't sleep on a bed as hard as this.

152. *Suggestions:* (*a*) start, rub, get, put, go, stand, feel, stretch. (*b*) Listen, hear, look, see, taste, smell. (*c*) slip, agree, Look, touch, think (believe). (*d*) take, go, get, put, Wait, drop, keep. (*e*) Come, send, hurry, run. (*f*) wonder, think (believe), know. (*g*) understand, mean. (*h*) tear, break, bend, stretch, twist, bite, press, draw. (*i*) give, throw, catch, turn, shake, pull. (*j*) jump, climb. (*k*) want, like, prefer. (*l*) stop, let, take (send). (*m*) hope, wish. [60]

162.   A group of people (*committee, government*, etc). may either be considered as a *body* (singular) or as a body of *persons* (plural). Either say '*A family has its* . . . ' or '*A family have their* . . . '; and do not make the same noun singular in one sentence and plural in the next. *The police* are generally plural. Regard *each* and *every* as singular. However, a sentence like 'Everyone wants their own way' is now very common.

166.   Do not stress *myself*, etc. in 166, but do so in 167.

172.   (*a*) it, me.   (*b*) myself, you, I, it.   (*c*) it, them.   (*d*) me, you, We, it, us.   (*e*) they, they, us.   (*f*) him, him.   (*g*) him, he, he, us.   (*h*) Who, it, it, ourselves.   (*i*) it, yourself.   (*j*) she, we, each other.   (*k*) they, us, We, one another.   (*l*) it, us, us, it.   (*m*) them, them, me.   (*n*) he, himself. (*o*) themselves, They.   (*p*) They, them.   (*q*) It. They. [50]

174.   (*a*) Say.   (*b*) Tell.   (*c*) Tell.   (*d*) say.   (*e*) Say.   (*f*) tell.   (*g*) tell. (*h*) say.   (*i*) say.   (*j*) tell.

183.   (*a*) enough, better.   (*b*) too, too much, less.   (*c*) very, always, well, sometimes, rather, faster.   (*d*) never, sometimes.   (*e*) nearly (almost), hardly.   (*f*) quite, nearly (almost, quite).   (*g*) late, still, early, already, yet. (*h*) nearer, hardly. [25]

186–188.   Use the Ordinary Present Tense in these exercises.

187.   The purpose of this exercise will perhaps be clearer if speaker A begins by saying to B 'I will tell you to do something. You do it, and at the same time tell me what you do'. Then A says to C 'I will tell B to do that again. As he does it, you tell me what he does'.

194.   Use the Present Continuous to give one of the kinds of emphasis specified in 194. Note that the author has avoided exercises which require the student to decide whether the Ordinary Present or the Present Continuous should be used. That choice depends very much on context and exactly what the speaker has in mind.

197.   See note 60. *Answers* In (*a*), use pattern A. In (*b*), use pattern B. In (*c*) A; (*d*) A; (*e*) B; (*f*) B; (*g*) A; (*h*) B; (*i*) B; (*j*) A.

198.   Do not use pronouns in the questions unless your audience knows who the pronouns refer to.

Suggestions for answers: Do you know the Joneses? Do you like them? Where do they live? Who drives their car? How do they drive? How does he go to his office? What do they do in the evening? Why do they go to the theatre? Who do they see there? How long does the play last? Do you speak Italian? Do you wear glasses? Do you smoke? Does your father smoke? When does he smoke a cigar? What do those people want? How do you spell 'hurry'? What does 'hurry' mean? How much does this book cost? How many pages do you read in an hour?

201.   Either *if* or *whether* could be used in *c, d, g, h* and *j*, but *if* is more likely in *c, d*, and *g*, and *whether* expresses the uncertainty in *h* and *j*.

212. This is an extract from a diary, not something especially written as a grammatical exercise. Note the alteration of Ordinary Present and Present Continuous Tense, the former giving a snap-shot or general view, the latter taking a motion picture and emphasising action in progress.

214. (a) he sees, she goes, he does, he says, etc. (b) There it is, there they are, shut it, etc. (c) be quiet. Move quietly. Don't make . . . I can hardly hear . . . (d) very well; pronounces, carefully; too quickly. (e) advice, advise, practise, practice. (f) lie, lay. (g) high enough, raise. (h) tell say, tell. (i) make, do. (j) show, show, explain, explain.

215. Be careful of *himself, themselves*.

216. Use the Present Continuous in a, b, the second part of c, in e, h, j; and the Ordinary Present in the first part of c, in d, f, g and i.

218. *Who is working in a factory? What is George doing? Where is he working?* etc. Note that stress and intonation in the answer would vary with the question.

220. (a) You speak English very well. (b) We can sometimes see the moon very clearly (or sometimes we can see . . .). (c) I can hardly answer that question myself. (d) That sentence does not quite make sense. (e) What do you do in the holidays? (f) We usually go to the sea in the summer (*or*, In the summer, we usually go). (g) Who sends his friends good wishes at Christmas? (h) You are not writing that carefully enough. (i) We often have no lessons on Saturday (*or*, On Saturday, we often have . . . *or*, Often, we have . . .). (j) Do not tell strangers your private business.

223. to, to, at, at, to, at, to, at, at, to. [10]

225. (a) at, to. (b) to, at. (c) at, to. (d) from, to. (e) from, to. (f) to, at. (g) to, at. (h) at, to. (i) from, from. (j) at, to. [20]

226. (a) at, to. (b) to, to. (c) to, at. (d) to, at. (e) to, at. (f) at, at, at. (g) to, at. [15]

228. (a) on, on, in, on, in (*or* on, *or* on top of), in, on, in, on. (b) off, off, out of, off, out of (*or* off), out of, off, out of, off. (c) in, on, in, on, in (*or* on). (d) into, out of, off, on to. (e) outside, inside, into (*or* inside). [30]

229. on, on to, into, into, in, into, in, into, into, on to. [10]

230. (a) at, on, in, at, at, at. (b) at, in, in. (c) on, in. (d) at, on, in. (e) in, at. (f) in. (g) at, in, at. [20]

232. along, across, by (or past), through, through, along, across, by, along, by. [10] Note *through the park* is better in this context, following into, which suggests a space; but *across* the park is also possible. Avoid *pass past*, because of the repetition of sound.

235. (a) with, without. (b) between, among. (c) round. (d) over. (e) above. (f) as far as, towards. (g) for. (h) beyond. (i) in front of. (j) behind, under. (k) with. (l) for, for. (m) for. (n) against, against. [20]

237. (a) at, in, on, since. (b) on, in. (c) in (or during), at. (d) after, before. (e) at, till, past, in (or during), through. (f) at, in, in (or during), at, on, till, past. (g) for, from, to (or till), during, through. (h) till, by, before, for. (i) in. (j) for. (k) at, before, till. (l) in, since, for. (m) for [40]

239. (a) by (*in every case*). (b) with (*in every case*). (c) about, on, by,

for, instead of. (*d*) about, about, on. (*e*) of, about, from, of (*or* about), for. (*f*) of, from. (*g*) of, from, of, from, by. (*h*) of, from, of, from. (*i*) as, like. (*j*) as, like. [40]

241.

(*a*) from.	(*b*) on.	(*c*) at.	(*d*) by.	(*e*) about.
(*f*) in.	(*g*) on.	(*h*) about.	(*i*) to	(*j*) with.
(*k*) of.	(*l*) to.	(*m*) of.	(*n*) from.	(*o*) for.
(*p*) with.	(*q*) of.	(*r*) at.	(*s*) for.	(*t*) to.
(*u*) from.	(*v*) for.	(*w*) in.	(*x*) at. (*y*) in.	(*z*) with.

242. (*a*) on, at, to, with, in, for. (*b*) for, round, on, of, on, between, in, past (*or* beyond). (*c*) from, across, to, opposite, for, in, from, to (*or* till), except, in, till, on. (*d*) with, to (*or* as far as), as far as. (*e*) Instead of, at, at, about, for. (*f*) for, like, of. (*g*) on, of, on. (*h*) with, about, of, in, of. (*i*) about, with, in, for, of. (*j*) over, under, above, of, below, in (*or* under *or* below), without, out of. (*k*) from, towards, on, of, along, on, through, up. (*l*) with, of, for, for, with, on. (*m*) at, in, on, for, till. (*n*) In, of, from, In, from, under, from, of, from, of. (*o*) on, from, with, from, for, for, about, on, of, till. (*p*) in, during, after. [100]

245. (*a*) out, back. (*b*) up. (*c*) down. (*d*) across. (*e*) over, through. (*f*) outside, away. (*g*) round. (*h*) back, down. (*i*) about, down. (*j*) off (*or* up). (*k*) away, back. (*l*) out, away. (*m*) by, up. (*n*) on, forwards, backwards. (*o*) up, upstairs. (*p*) over, over. (*q*) afterwards. (*r*) downwards. [30]

246. (*a*) down to. (*b*) across to. (*c*) along to. (*d*) round to. (*e*) back to. (*f*) up on. (*g*) down on. (*h*) over to the other side. (*i*) through to the other side. (*j*) by on the other side. [10]

248. (*a*) on, up. (*b*) up (*or* in), out. (*c*) up, up, on, up. (*d*) off (*or* out). (*e*) out, out. (*f*) out. (*g*) out, out. (*h*) up. [15]

250.

(*a*) B.	(*b*) B.	(*c*) A.	(*d*) A.	(*e*) B.
(*f*) A.	(*g*) A.	(*h*) B.	(*i*) B.	(*j*) 246.
(*k*) A.	(*l*) B.	(*m*) 246.	(*n*) B.	(*o*) A.
(*p*) A.	(*q*) B.	(*r*) B.	(*s*) B.	(*t*) B.
(*u*) A.	(*v*) B.	(*w*) A.	(*x*) A.	(*y*) B.

257. In the 3rd person, verbs ending in d or t, e.g. *attend*, *visit*, have an extra syllable in the past, not in the present; verbs ending in a hissing sound, e.g. *advise*, *brush*, *change*, *dance*, *use*, *watch*, have an extra syllable in the present, not in the past. Note the spelling of: *applied*, *begged*, *fitted*, *referred*, *suffered*, *travelled*, *visited*, *wrapped*.

267. *Answers:* (*a*) shut, put, took, did not shut, was, went, came, opened, found, turned. (*b*) woke up, lay, read, got up, washed, got dressed, had breakfast, left, walked, bought, caught, paid, gave, took, was. (*c*) was not, were you? how was, how were, was, wasn't it? That was. Those were, weren't they? (*d*) was, stayed; wrote, did you get (*or* receive); have you heard? Did you hear? hurt, have not been able; was, died; Have we done (finished)? did (*or* finished).

268. *Proceed as follows:* (*a*) Does your mother make your clothes herself? She used to make our clothes herself, but she doesn't now. (*b*) I always went to school by bus. Do you always go, etc. I used to go, etc., but I don't now, etc.

269. *Specimen answer:* Every day, I rest . . . It is now 9 o'clock. I am not busy. I am resting. I have been resting for one hour. What have I been doing? (Answer) Suppose it is now 10. I am not tired, etc.

270. *Answers:* (*a*) Because the sun has been shining on it. (*b*) Because I have been running up and down stairs. (*c*) He has been working too hard. (*d*) No wonder: she has been practising it for six months. (*e*) She was practising a piece of music. (*f*) He was working too hard. (*g*) How long have you been learning English? I have been learning it for . . . (*h*) We have been waiting. What were we doing? We were waiting. (*i*) I am doing an exercise (answering a question). What were you doing? I was . . . (*j*) What have you been doing? I have been doing this exercise (answering these questions).

273. (*a*) We gave a party. We had invited a lot of people. Had we invited everybody? No, we hadn't . . . (*b*) There was enough to eat. We had ordered plenty of food. Had we ordered everything? No, we hadn't . . . (*c*) Last year we stayed . . . We had usually rented a cottage before. Had we always rented (or stayed) . . . ? etc. (*d*) Last year, my father caught . . . He had never been ill before. Had he ever been ill (had he always been well) before? No, he had never been ill (he had always been well) before.

274. (*a*) arrived, had left already (*or* had already left). (*b*) arrived, had left. (*c*) met, had not met. (*d*) had never seen, I recognised. (*e*) knew, had met. (*f*) found, had fallen. (*g*) had lain, was. (*h*) had had, felt. (*i*) reached, had travelled, had climbed, had ever explored. [20]

275. The model for 275 is the past of the model for 270. Proceed as follows: (*a*) Why was the wall so hot? Because the sun had been shining on it. (*b*) Why were you . . . ? Because I had been running . . . (*c*) Was your father . . . Yes, he had been working . . . (*d*) Mary played . . . she had been practising . . . (*e*) What had M. been doing three weeks before? She had been . . . (*f*) What had your father been doing? He had been . . . (*g*) We were learning . . . Suppose you had started two years before. How long had you been learning till then? (*h*) We were waiting . . . We had got here (*or* there) half an hour before, so we had been waiting . . . What had we been doing half an hour before? (*i*) What were you doing? What had you been (or were you) doing? (*j*) It was time . . . What had you been doing for the last ten minutes?

278. *Answers:* I will be studying for three more hours. What will you be doing? etc.

279. *Answer:* (I'll tell you tomorrow) I will have seen it, heard it, met him, written it, thought about it, by then.

280. There are, however, other uses of *would*. These will be dealt with in Chapter 7.

283. (*a*) *What are we having?* (something is already started). '*What are we going to have*' is possible (present indications), but not necessary. 'What

will we have' and 'What do we have' are also possible, but do not fit so well into the context.

(*b*) *Who is coming?* (something is obviously planned).

(*c*) *You are going to break.* (The 'present indications' are clear.) '*You will break*', emphasising the future event, is equally possible. '*You are breaking*', as a reference of future action, would be wrong; no one has arranged it.

(*d*) *I am going to sell* (my present intentions tell me what will happen). '*I am selling*' is also possible, though it might be taken as an example of 190 or 192.

(*e*) *The roof is going to collapse.* (Present indications are clear.) '*The roof is collapsing*' as a reference to *future* action would be wrong, as in (*c*).

(*f*) *I'll carry.* (The question of intentions, arrangements, etc. does not arise. There is no time for it anyway.)

(*g*) *I'll open.* (There are no present indications of what the future will bring, since I don't know what you want.)

(*h*) *we're going to have* (emphasis of 'present indications').

(*i*) *I'll be.* ('*I'm going to be*' is also possible, but unnecessary.)

(*j*) *What are you doing?* (emphasis on plans) '*What are you going to do*' is also possible (emphasis on present intentions).

(*k*) *leave, arrive* (according to programme).

(*l*) *You're going to have* (judging from the present indications). *You'll have* (emphasis on future) is also possible.

(*m*) '*will take place*' or '*takes place*'; but '*is taking place*'; '*is going to* . . .' are both also possible, though unnecessary: the plain statement of future or of programme is more business-like.

(*n*) '*will not be*' (plain business-like statement). '*He is not going to be*' is also possible, but unnecessary and would result in undesirable repetition in view of the second sentence, which should be '*He is going abroad*' (He has arranged it: that is why he will not be there).

(*o*) *I am seeing him.* (I have arranged an appointment.) '*I am going to see*,' or '*I'll see*', are also possible.

284. (*a*) went. (*b*) got. (*c*) brought. (*d*) was (*or* were). (*e*) were. (*f*) was (or were). (*g*) had heard. (*h*) would ask. (*i*) had asked. (*j*) hadn't.

286. (*a*) could not, did he think, we did not know. (*b*) I promised I would not forget. I hoped you would believe me. (*c*) was, It had been. (*d*) Who could tell what the next day would bring? (*e*) were, had been shining. (*f*) was, I thought . . . he felt . . . we had done. (*g*) was getting. I was sure there would be . . . had already returned . . . were fastening. (*h*) was, had been destroyed, it would take. [25]

287. (*a*) have been dealing, I hope you have not forgotten (or will not forget). (*b*) did you get, asked, put, felt, remembered, told, woke, thought, heard, were, crept, opened, listened, heard, began, caught, someone had left, fell, I wonder, did not hear, picked myself up, found myself, was, a man was standing (*or* stood). He shone, saw, was, asked (or said), Are, Did you hurt (Have you hurt), came, was, think, forgot, thanked, shut,

came (*or* went), slept, woke. What did you do . . . , I said (answered), could not find, is, will fall over it.

(*c*) are doing, (*or* have been doing). We will not do (won't do), we have done. Have you got (*or* Did you get).

288. 1. I have borne it . . . 2. But he beat me. 3. It began . . . 4. I bent it . . . 5. It has just bitten (me). 6. It blew the roof off. 7. How did you break it? 8. Yes, I brought one. 9. He has burnt it already. 10. I bought it . . . 11. Mary chose it . . . 12. It cost . . . 13. I cut it . . . 14 They dug it . . . 15. Yes, I drew one . . . 16. I haven't dreamt . . . 17. I have drunk it up already. 18. I have driven one for years . . . 19. I have eaten . . . 20. They flew across in . . . 21. I have already given it to him (given it to him already). 22. I grew it . . . 23. I hung it . . . 24. he hid it. 25. We held it . . . 26. We knew them . . . 27. They laid it . . . 28. Yes, they led it. 29. Somebody lent them one. 30. I let it out . . . 31. I lay down on the deck. 32. I lost it . . . 33. I meant exactly . . . 34. I put it on . . . 35. I have rung it twice . . . 36. I ran . . . 37. I sold it for . . . 38. They set out at day-break. 39. Yes, I shook it hard. 40. I shot it with a rifle. 41. It sank . . . 42. I've spent it all . . . 43. I haven't spoilt it (*or* I won't). 44. I spread them out in the . . . 45. it sprang out . . . 46. Nobody stole it (*or* has stolen it): it is still in your pocket. 47. I have struck two . . . 48. I told him to drive . . . 49. Both swam across it. 50. I've worn it . . .

291. *Answers* to (*a*), (*b*), and other questions can easily be found in the text. Note: (*c*) No, he had never left his own country before. (*f*) Yes, he knew it very well. (*h*) The friend asked him how he was. (*i*) 'How are you?' (*j*) The friend next asked him whether he was enjoying himself. (*k*) 'Are you enjoying yourself?' (*l*) The visitor said he was feeling well. (*n*) He had gone for a walk round the streets. (*o*) 'I went for a walk round the streets and found myself at Victoria Station.' (*r*) He saw a train come in. (*s*) The doors swung outward as the train came nearer and nearer. (*t*) The train came nearer and nearer to where he was standing. (*u*) They jumped out while the train was still moving.

294. *Answers.* Put (*a*) and (*f*) together; (*b*) and (*p*); (*c*) and (*w*); (*d*) and (*v*); (*e*) and (*r*); (*g*) and (*q*); (*h*) and (*l*); (*i*) and (*n*); (*j*) and (*t*); (*k*) and (*m*); (*o*) and (*s*); (*u*) and (*x*).

298. (*a*) from, to, drive, in, between, passes, through, on, on, beyond. (*b*) am leaving (or *leave*, or *will leave*, or *am going to leave*), for, in, have not started, yet, at, am waiting, am starting (or *start*, or *will start*, or *am going to start*), at, know, will arrive, at, in, started, off. (*c*) am driving, left, ago, am going, away from, is travelling, towards, is moving, along, in front. (*d*) only, on, across, over, under, see, are riding, along, beside, drive, past, behind. (*e*) have been driving, since, for, have already completed, will drive (or *will be driving*), for, till (or *until*), by, to. (*f*) Have I arrived at Z yet? No, not yet, have arrived, arrived, ago, have travelled, have been driving, for. (*g*) left, at, passed, through, at, was driving, was still travelling, with, had left, before. (*h*) was, at, knew, would arrive, in, was, had travelled, had been driving, at, had not started, yet, was waiting. (*i*) was

coming, saw, were riding, passed. (*j*) I drove, to, without, did not come, with, had come.

299. *Possible answers:* (*a*) George is still in bed. (*b*) He has been awake for two hours. (*c*) Mary is not awake yet. (*d*) You don't eat very much (or *a lot*). (*e*) Some people eat too much. (*f*) There are too many people in (or *on*) this boat. (*g*) That is my firm belief. (*h*) Breathe deeply. (*i*) He works hard. (*j*) She makes her own clothes. (*k*) I'm asking you his name. (*l*) This material is called nylon. (*m*) Get your guest a chair. (*n*) You do not practise enough. (*o*) I (or *we* or *you*) cannot drink this tea. (*p*) George always disobeys me. (*q*) A wooden building. (*r*) Your business train. (*s*) Take these things away. (*t*) Let's leave this place. (*u*) I ask you whether (or *if*) this is the right road. (*v*) My room is below yours but not right under (or *underneath*) it. (*w*) I saw John when I was coming (or *going*) home. (*x*) Please explain to us the meaning of this sentence. (*y*) It's late: it's time we stopped.

300. *Answers:* (*a*) We usually go into the country on Sundays. (*or* On Sundays, we usually go into the country). (*b*) Both the old blue Persian rugs in this room are my uncle's. (*c*) Who dug up all those tomato plants in the garden yesterday? (*d*) They have not put these pictures up on the wall carefully enough. (*e*) Did you see the fireworks last night? They were wonderful, weren't they? (*f*) A professor with white hair was talking but his students were all walking about and nobody was listening to him. (*g*) Before James Hudson came here, we had never heard anything about him. (*h*) 'Have you worked out that problem already?' she asked. 'Not yet,' we answered. (*or* 'Have you worked that problem out . . .) (*i*) She asked us if we had worked it out properly. (*j*) 'Is there anybody there?' said the guide, knocking on the door with his stick.

INDEX

List of Tables

INDEX

Subjects and words treated.

Numbers refer to paragraphs and exercises (or, when stated, to tables)